SHADOW OF THE BEAST

First published by Hodder Children's Books, 2002.
First published in the Hodder Literature series, 2005,
by Hodder Murray, a member of the Hodder Headline Group,
338 Euston Road, London NW1 3BH.

| Impression number | 10 | 9 | 8 | 7 | 6 | 5 | 4 | 3 | 2 | 1 |
| Year | | 2010 | 2009 | 2008 | 2007 | 2006 | 2005 | | | |

ISBN-10   0 340 89988 3
ISBN-13   9 780340 899885

A catalogue record for this title is available from the British Library

Typeset in Bembo by Servis Filmsetting Ltd, Manchester.
Printed in Great Britain by CPI Bath.

Orders: please contact Bookpoint Ltd, 130 Milton Park, Abingdon,
Oxon OX14 4SB. Telephone: (44) 01235 827720. Fax: (44) 01235
400454. Lines are open from 9.00 am to 6.00 pm, Monday to
Saturday, with a 24-hour message answering service.
Visit our website at www.hoddereducation.co.uk

Shadow of the Beast

Maggie Pearson

HODDER LITERATURE

www.hodderliterature.co.uk

To order **Shadow of the Beast** or any of the other books in the Hodder Literature series, please contact Bookpoint on 01235 827720.

For all the unsung heroes

If it be now, 'tis not to come; if it be not to come, it will be now;
    If it be not now, yet it will come; the readiness is all.

William Shakespeare, *Hamlet*

One

All the boy knew was that he was afraid.

Afraid of what?

A thing without a name.

Afraid of every passing shadow, the screech owl's cry, the fox's bark and the pitter-pattering of tiny feet among the undergrowth.

At night when they lay down to sleep, fear gnawed at his insides worse than any hunger.

In the morning, breaking camp, setting off again while the world was still licking itself into shape out of the grey mists of dawn, fear dogged his footsteps, closer than his own shadow. Fear peering wide-eyed over his shoulder at the greater fear that lay ahead.

How long had they been travelling? Days? Weeks? He couldn't remember a time before.

'Where are we going?'

'That's for me to know,' the blind man said, 'and for you to find out!' He gave a sudden bark of laughter which sent the forest birds into a fluttering panic. The boy found himself unexpectedly alone as the path they were following took a twist around a bramble thicket. He hitched up the bundle on his back, the blankets, the cooking pot and tripod, the harp and the ceremonial feathered cloak, and trotted the next few steps to catch up.

'Why do I have to carry everything?' he grumbled. 'Why can't you lend a hand?'

'Because I am a Bard of the Silver Branch and you are a boy of no account that I found crying by the roadside.'

'Huh!' The bedroll was morphing into a snake, trying to squirm out from under his arm, and the harp had turned affectionate, its strings nibbling at his left ear. 'And what did your last slave die of?' the boy muttered mutinously.

'Of a curse!' the man spat back.

'Pull the other one! People don't die of a curse!'

'Depends who's doing the cursing.'

'Oh, don't tell me. Let me guess.'

'Always complaining, he was. Thought I'd give him something to complain about, like a plague of boils. Rather overdid it, I'm afraid. He was called Wiglaf, too.'

Through gritted teeth the boy muttered to himself (not that he believed a word of that stuff about a curse, but still you can't be too careful), 'My name is *not* Wiglaf.'

'Didn't say his name *was* Wiglaf. *Called* Wiglaf, that's what I said.'

Sunlight filtered green by the forest leaves leached the colour from their faces till they looked like ghosts. Like ghosts they moved through the moist, misty marshes, where men in flat-bottomed boats were slowly, rhythmically gathering reeds, or else sat motionless, eel-spear at the ready, never once lifting their heads to see the two of them pass by.

Following a blind man through the marshes, where a single false step— He must be mad. 'How do you know the right way to go?'

'I can hear it! I can smell it! Come on, Wiglaf!'

I am not Wiglaf. Wiglaf is Not – My – Name! What kind of a name was Wiglaf? Short-arsed and thick as cold porridge, with a sad haircut. Whereas he was . . . his name was . . . *OK, then, call me Wiglaf, see if I care!* He hitched up the bedroll again and slung the cooking pot and trivet either side of his shoulder in an effort to stop their ceaseless clank-clank-clanking.

They came to a kind of settlement. Too big to be called a village, not organized enough for a town. No streets, just houses set down anywhere, timber-framed, with thatched roofs pitched so low there was no room left for windows.

'Wiglaf! Where are you? Here, boy! Come!' The man's hand fastened round his wrist like a claw. 'Now it's your turn to guide me.'

So he threaded a path for them both round the cooking fires, past the potters and dyers and metalworkers. Past women sitting in the watery sunlight, spinning, feeding babies, grinding corn. Pigs, chickens and dogs rooted amongst the rubbish. Barefoot children seemed to be everywhere.

Long-haired, moustachioed, loud-voiced men tramped past them, boots squelching through the mud and muck.

What must it be like, to be blind in such a place? Voices calling, snatches of song. The sound of a hammer on metal. Plus unidentified hisses, squeaks, rumbles, clatters . . . A powerful stink of leather, damp sheep, pigs, dogs and garden compost all mingling with the cooking smells.

'Wait!' The man's fingertips bit deeper into his arm. The boy opened his eyes and gasped. The building towering in front of them cast them into cold shadow. It was built of solid trunks of wood, as if the trees had drawn together to form a wall, and topped with row upon row of wide, tiered gables, each crowned with antlers.

The bard stretched out the hand that held his poet's staff and sniffed the air. 'Lead me forward!' he demanded. 'Closer, boy! Closer!' Until he was able to let go of the boy's wrist, reach out and touch the nearest doorpost, running his fingers over the carvings that spiralled down it. 'Yes,' he said quietly. 'This is the place.'

The boy felt the fear move suddenly nearer, resting a cold hand on his shoulder. 'You must describe it to me, Wiglaf.'

'Describe what?'

'All of it!' A terrible, yearning hunger in his voice. The man had not always been blind. He raised his staff to knock.

4

And the boy knew that once that door was opened there would be no going back. With all the breath in his body he cried out, '*No!*'

Knock! Knock!

No!

Knock! Knock! The knocking came again, but quietly, more of a tap! tap!

'Troy?' A woman's voice, hesitant, enquiring. 'Are you awake, Troy?'

Far, far away, at the end of a long, dark tunnel, he saw the bedroom door edge open, and a figure framed by the light. 'Troy?' Flo's face swam into focus. 'Brought you a cup of tea.'

The cup floating towards him was blue, with a chain of daisies round the rim and a custard cream perched in the saucer.

'It's gone nine!' Flo said brightly. 'I let you sleep in for a bit, then I heard you moving about, so I thought . . . since I'd just made one for us.'

He felt as if he hadn't slept at all, a stiffness in his legs like he'd been walking all night long. He could feel the bruises on his wrist where the blind man had gripped it, though there was nothing to see.

'Shall I draw back the curtains?'

'If you want.' Somewhere beyond the stripped pine wardrobe and chest of drawers, the flowered wallpaper and the autumn sunlight dappling the curtains, there was still the shadow of that other world.

Daylight streamed in, but the after-image of his

dream still lingered. The same one he used to dream when he was in the hospital. Except this time they seemed to have reached the place they were heading for. This time he had been on the point of stepping through that door, into a world of dim light and smoky shadows; smells of leather and roast meat and air breathed many times over. The murmur of men's voices. A sudden burst of laughter. Like the pub where they'd stopped off – when was it? Where was it? They were on the road to— He fingered the long scar on his forehead (almost hidden by his hair now), but the memory slid away and he was left with Flo, turning from the window, pushing a wayward strand of grey hair back behind her ear. 'I heard you cry out as I came up the stairs. Bad dream, was it?'

'No.' He didn't want sympathy. Or company. 'I'm fine.'

'Good.' She stood twisting the wedding ring on her finger as if, after all these years, it had suddenly grown too tight.

Downstairs a bell jangled. A murmur of voices came from under her feet. Flo smiled, relieved.

'Duty calls. Doris isn't in to help me in the shop this morning. She's gone to the hospital with her leg. And Stan's out the back. He won't have heard the bell. Never does these days, if he can help it,' she added half to herself. Then the smile was back in place: 'He's got a bit of a surprise for you later. Anyway. Come down when you're ready.'

6

'OK.' He nodded towards the tea cooling on the beside table. 'Thanks, Flo.'

'My pleasure. It's nice to have you back, Troy.'

After she'd gone, he snuggled down again under the covers. Troy. His name was Troy, not Wiglaf. Never Wiglaf. *I'm Troy*.

Armed with the knowledge of his own, true name, he closed his eyes, letting himself slide back again into that other world.

Two

In the mead-hall the feasting was as good as over. The smoky lights were burning low. Sleepy warriors chatted, fell into a doze, then jerked awake again, picked themselves another scrap of meat off the bone, and carried on talking from where they'd left off. House slaves moved quietly among them, trimming candles, stoking the braziers with fresh charcoal, refilling cups, clearing dishes, tossing scraps to the dogs, who fought as if that mouthful was all that lay between them and sure starvation. Children, unnaturally bright-eyed and heavy with sleep, were summoned by proud fathers from the women's quarters to strut their stuff.

Then, as if at some secret signal, servants, dogs, children were all gone, and the central space swept clear. From his place at the King's high table the Bard of the Silver Branch stepped down, silently counting off the paces till he stood centre stage, then turning carefully, just as the two of them had rehearsed it, to face the King. He struck his staff three times on the wooden floor. 'Listen!' he demanded, not loudly, yet the conversation slowly began to die. 'Listen!' he whispered, softer still. Then, turning, used his staff to draw a circle in the air around him, with a tinkling of tiny silver bells which reached out to the furthest corners of the hall, trailing a ripple of utter silence in its wake.

Someone had brought him his harp and a stool to sit on.

'Listen!' he murmured, fingers flickering over the harpstrings, 'and I will tell you a tale of the hero-time, long ago. The world needed heroes then. For there were monsters that prowled by night and lurked in the deep, dark, dismal places – in the misty marshes and in the frozen forests and in the hidden hollows of men's minds.

'Listen! And you shall hear the hell-hag's spawn slide from his oozy bed and go pad-padding across the marshland.

'Listen! And you shall hear the song of the sea – taste the salt spray – sway with the swing of the keel as the hero takes the whales' road. Beowulf!'

'Beowulf!' The echo reverberated round the hall, gathering to a cheer of '*Beowulf!*' They thumped the tables and drank to Beowulf till even the old King on his throne jerked awake, looked round as if to say, 'Where am I? Who am I? And who are you?' Then, remembering his manners, drank too and, forgetting that the bard was blind, nodded graciously for him to carry on before settling to sleep again.

In his soft, western lilt, the bard continued: 'It was in the time that Hrothgar was King . . .'

'Hrothgar!' the man on Troy's left rumbled approvingly.

'He was a good king, favoured by Fortune, strong in battle and wise in peace. Warriors and heroes flocked to his court until the mead-hall was full to overflowing. So Hrothgar ordered the building of a new hall, where there would be room for all. Heorot! A hall to rival Asgard, home of the gods!'

'Hrothgar! Good man!' murmured the warrior on Troy's right.

'Rival the gods, though,' said the man on his left, the two of them talking across him, as if he wasn't really there. 'Hic! Gods might not like it.'

'Drink to him, anyway.'

'Hrothgar. Hic! Why not?'

The blind bard's voice sang on. It was a voice made for enchantments, weaving a living picture out of the fire-smoke and the dancing shadows. 'From the northlands he fetched pinewood, sweet cedar from the south and the scented sandalwood, and had it carved with trees, flowers, game birds, deer, wild boar and hunting dogs that ran and leapt in the flickering firelight.'

Troy remembered what the bard had said as he was leading him round: 'You think because I am blind that I see nothing! What I see in here,' – tapping his own forehead – 'here, in my mind's eye, is better – finer! – than anything you see with your two. Inside here, boy, I am a magician! Transforming the everyday into something wonderful, rich and strange.' It was this place the blind man was recreating. And either there was something in the mead, or it was the harp-song and the lilting voice in harmony, or the glamour was all in the willingness of so many listeners together to see the world remade – but this was the place! Heorot! The hall fit for heroes. The wooden floor transformed into a dazzling mosaic. The homespun tapestries that lined the walls peopled with moving images that acted out the battle-glories of Hrothgar the King, and of his father, and of his father's father, and his father too, Scyld Scefing, who began with nothing and won himself a kingdom!

'Scyld Scefing! Good man!'

'Drink to him?'

'Why not? Hic!'

From the heroes' hall of Heorot the sounds of feasting carried far into the night, over the empty huts and through the forest and out into the marshland.

'Deep in the marshes,' the blind man murmured, the harp-song shifting to a minor key, 'deep in the misty marshes, the slime seethed and shifted . . .'

It was just a story. The boy knew it was a story. But out in the darkness, beyond the firelight, the fear that stalked him was real, a living thing. Slowly, out of the foul waters of the marsh, out of the stinking slime, his terror took shape, and came, death dripping from its fingers' ends, pad-padding towards the heroes' hall. At last it had a name. Grendel.

★   ★   ★

11

'How long?' the blind man asked. 'How long had Grendel been sleeping? Ages – long ages. Fathoms deep. Something had woken him. Music and laughter. A sound that would not let him rest again but drew him up, out of the filthy waters of the wasteland. At the forest's edge, Grendel stopped. He hated the light. So he skulked in the shadows until the fires faded and the men wrapped themselves in their cloaks and settled to sleep. Then Grendel crept forward and peered into the hall. He looked around. He sniffed the air and smelled man-meat. Man-meat was good – and Grendel was hungry.

'He picked up the nearest, bit off his head and ate him, skin, bone, belt, buckles and boots and all. Yes! Man-meat was good. Grendel took another . . . and another . . .

'Morning came, sun rising, marsh-mist thinning, warriors waking to a world changed for ever! Thirty men gone! Slain in their sleep, without a second to snatch up their swords. Their blood scattered everywhere: over the carved pillars and the tapestries, the benches inlaid with gold and ivory, and the patterned floor. But where were their bodies?

'Nothing remained,' the blind man mourned. 'Not one scrap of flesh or shard of bone over which to say their funeral rites and give their poor souls rest.

'What enemy had done this? What enemy could come and go so silently? They searched the forest, the roads and the seashore. Took boats along the streams and rivulets that criss-crossed the marshes. But found no sign.

'That night they feasted again in Heorot. Men had died in that place, but the living must eat. So they ate together, but quietly. There was no laughter and no music in Hrothgar's hall that night. Yet Grendel heard them. Out of the marshlands he came slithering, sliding, to satisfy the hunger that would not let him rest.

'They barred the door before they lay down to sleep, but bolts and bars could not stop Grendel. With one blow, he thrust open the door. Awake! Awake!'

Heads of the listeners turned as one towards the door of the mead-hall.

'Men started up, rubbing sleep from their eyes, as one great, taloned hand reached out and seized the nearest victim. At once the rest attacked him—'

Hands reached for swords, spears, axes, whatever, while the harp sang a song of panic and discord.

The blind man shook his head. 'Grendel brushed them aside, like flies on a summer's day, and took his pick from the bodies scattered there.'

Sleepily, seeing the door still safely shut, they remembered where they were, met each others' eyes with a wry smile and took another drink.

'Now men who had stood firm against the enemy in twenty battles flung down their weapons and fled for their lives. Cowering under benches and tables, shivering behind tapestries, trembling in corners, Grendel gouged them out.'

Not me! Not me! I'm not ready yet to die! Troy curled himself up into a bundle, crouching, hovering between worlds. Part of him knew he was safe, yet he could smell the monster's foetid breath, feel the cold talons fasten round him. Eyes blazing out of the dark and a roaring in his ears. Somewhere deep down inside, he knew it was all – all! – just a dream, but he couldn't move a muscle. Such a weight bearing down on his chest! He couldn't breathe.

Then came a brilliant white light, and figures in silhouette bending over him. 'I think he's coming round. What's his name?'

Troy! I'm Troy! No sound coming out. He still couldn't move. And the beast was crushing the life out of him.

'It's OK. Settle down now. You're going to be OK.'

And then he was awake again. The room looked strange. Flowered wallpaper he recognized. Sunlight through the curtains, stripped pine wardrobe and chest of drawers, but in all the wrong places. It took him a moment to realize that he was lying sideways, across the bed. *I am here. I am Troy.* Flo downstairs in the shop and Stan out the back. All the rest, just a dream.

He slipped off the bed and took a good look at himself in the mirror. *This is me.* Eyes, ears, mouth – check. Nose not quite as I remember it, looks a bit bent, *but still me.* He pushed back the hair from his forehead so he could get a good look at the scar. Like someone had sliced off the top of his head, then neatly stitched it back in place. Frankenstein's monster.

He went to the window to check out the view. Below him he could see Stan, spider-thin, his long, grey hair pulled back in a ponytail. He was unscrewing the doors of the little pine cupboard they'd collected from the stripper's on the way back from the hospital yesterday. Behind him lay the lawn and the vegetable patch with its freshly-turned earth and neat rows of parsnips and celery, sprouts, cabbages and leeks. Beyond, the treetops blazed with autumn fire, yellow-gold and red-gold flickering in the breeze against a hazy blue sky.

The sight of the old swing at the corner of the lawn brought back a sudden memory of himself at three years old. He could feel the hard wooden seat tilting under him as Dad lifted him up. 'Up you come, Tel!' Little legs dangling. 'Hold on tight!' And he did – he did! because that was what Dad told him to do – though the rough ropes hurt his palms. And shrieked with pleasure each time the wind sucked the breath out of him as Dad pushed him higher and higher. Startled seagulls watched, wheeling overhead, expecting him to come flying up to join them any minute.

Then Mum appeared on the back doorstep and her face froze into a mask of panic. 'Ray, no! You're pushing him too high!'

'He's fine!'

'He'll fall! He'll fall!' And Troy began screaming too, terrified by the look on her face and the whirlwind of angry voices spinning round him. The swing bruised his leg as Mum snatched him off before Dad had properly stopped it. Her chunky necklace bored into his cheek. Troy bellowed louder, scarlet-faced, and kicked and kicked till she let him slip to the ground so she could see to her cream jersey dress. Ugh! The mess his muddy shoes had made! And Flo, lovely Flo! soft as a feather pillow and smelling of Imperial Leather and fresh-baked bread, came and gathered him up and carried him through to the shop, leaving his mum and dad still bickering.

Customers smiled at him. 'Who's this, then?'

'This is Ray's boy.'

'My goodness! I'd never have known him: he's grown so since I last saw him.'

Flo, as proud as any proper gran, wiping his tears away before lifting him down off the counter.

'Do you remember where the cat food is, Troy? Off you go, then, and fetch me four tins for Miss Moffatt, while I carve her a quarter-pound of ham. Four tins. Two for Dusty, two for Daisy. Two and two makes . . . ?'

'Four o'course!' He fetched the tins back, one at a time, reaching on tiptoe to slide them on to the counter.

'Got a helper today, I see,' nodded Captain Peasgrove.

'Ray's boy.'

'I'm Ray's boy.'

Always Ray's; never Ray and Sheila's.

From outside the bedroom window, Stan's voice floated up, singing as he hand-sanded the top of the old pine cupboard. Where other people might whistle or hum, Stan would sing. '*Here I sit on Butternut Hill. Who'd deny me to cry my fill? Every tear would turn a mill . . .*'

Troy suddenly felt his own eyes filling with tears. He brushed them away. Do something. Anything. He pulled on his clothes, jeans and sweatshirt. Trainers, still laced from yesterday. The tea in the cup was cold and unappetizing, the taste of mead still bitter-sweet in his mouth, so he tipped the tea away, down the washbasin. Wiglaf-like, he rubbed at his teeth and gums with his finger, swilling out with a mouthful of water before he noticed the toothbrush and toothpaste lying there.

He hurried downstairs and caught Flo in a rare moment of stillness, dishmop poised over the breakfast washing-up.

Outside, Stan was still singing, '*Till he comes back I'll rue the day . . .*'

'I haven't heard him sing that,' Flo said quietly, 'not in a month of Sundays.' She turned back to the sink for a spot of GBH on the frying pan.

Breakfast was laid ready for him on the table. Grapefruit juice and packets of cereal. Bread-and-butter soldiers lined up ready for action. Toaster plugged in. Marmalade, honey and three flavours of jam.

'Just cereal's fine, Flo.' There was an emptiness deep inside him, but it wasn't hunger.

'You've been in hospital. You need building up. It's no trouble just to boil an egg.' She popped it into the pan. 'Doesn't matter if you don't finish it.'

He sipped at the juice. It tasted of nothing. Worse than nothing, vinegar and vomit. He set the glass down again and concentrated on arranging the jars in front of him in different ways, trying to get the labels to match up.

The shop bell rang.

'I'll go,' offered Troy.

'No, no! You stay there. Finish your breakfast.' Flo stripped off her rubber gloves and made for the connecting door. 'Just take it out when the timer goes. The egg? Three and a half minutes, right?'

'Right.'

As soon as the door swung to behind her, he slid off his chair and out of the opposite door into the open air, moving silent as a shadow. Stan, with his back turned, was still singing quietly, sadly, to himself as he worked, '*Shule, shule, shul'agra . . .*'

Once safely out in the lane and hidden by the laurel hedge, Troy bent to retie his trainers. Then he set off, walking. Away from the kitchen, the snug warmth of the Aga, the air struck chill, straight to the bone. Clear blue sky above, but the sun might as well have been the moon for all the warmth to be wrung from it. He should have brought his coat. He could hear Mum saying it: 'Don't forget your coat!'

18

Which was a good enough reason for leaving it behind.

He stuck his hands in his pockets and walked on, head down, still keeping one eye open in case he saw someone he knew. Ready to turn away and pretend he hadn't noticed.

But there was no one. No sign of human life, but a garden fork abandoned beside a half-empty string bag of bulbs and an optimistic line of washing, hanging cold and lifeless. Water droplets dripped from every roof and branch, as if the world was quietly dissolving in a flood of dusty tears.

Three

There were no elms any more in the village of Elm Green, not since the Dutch elm disease. The 'green' had never been more than a muddy hump, worn bare of grass by people stamping their feet warm while they waited for the one bus out per day. A scatter of tumbledown cottages, two squat, grey Victorian terraces and a red-brick council estate with pebble-dash bungalows for the old folk. One church, St Edmund's, not specially old or interesting. One pub, The New Inn, ditto. One post office cum general store. That was Elm Green.

But for Troy, every time he came back to the place where his dad more or less grew up, it had always been like snuggling into a favourite jumper on a cold morning.

Only now it was like the jumper didn't quite fit any more. Was it something not right with the world, or something wrong with him?

He kept on walking till he was out of the village and on towards the sea, still walking, past one ploughed field . . . one field of soggy sheep . . . one threadbare meadow. After that there was nothing but

rough scrub, stunted bushes and clumps of skeleton
blades of grass whispering together. The road
dwindled to a dirt track sloping upwards, soft soil
dragging at his feet. By the time he reached the top his
legs were so weary, he just let them fold under him
and sat with a thump on the damp, greyish sand.

In front of him the beach swept down more gently
than the slope he'd climbed. The grass grew more
spare, half buried in drifting sand, till the sand became
shingle, sloping to the water's edge, white-toothed
wavelets nibbling at the edges of the land. Coastal
erosion. Awesome. Chances were that in a hundred
years all this bit of coastline would be gone. In two
hundred the village itself, maybe. Nothing left but the
sea.

And where would he be then?

They said he'd almost died. He didn't remember.

They told him he'd been unconscious for weeks –
long enough for the broken bones to heal.

But he didn't remember breaking any bones.

Troy shivered. He ought to go back. The cold wind
nipped at his nose and ear lobes. He was feeling the
damp through the seat of his jeans, but still he sat.

It would be OK when Dad came. 'I'll come for
you,' he'd promised. Troy could hear him saying it; he
just couldn't quite picture the time or the place. Dad
would get things sorted. All Troy had to do was wait.

Someone was walking their dog along the beach,
too far away for him to make out whether the figure
was male or female.

Away against the blue horizon a white sail skimmed the water. He thought at first it was a stray cloud, then watched as it grew steadily larger, heading for the shore, till he could make out the splashes from the dip and sweep of oars. Five, six? No – seven oarsmen along this side, times two makes fourteen. They were long-haired and bearded, and dressed in leather and sheepskin, like the warriors in his dream. The fifteenth man stood at the stern, legs braced against the dip and swing of the keel, strong hands gripping the huge wooden tiller.

The steersman shouted an order and the rowers rested on their oars, letting the onward rush carry the boat till it grounded on the shingle. Without a glance in Troy's direction they vaulted waist-deep into the ice-cold water and, with much heaving and hoing, dragged the boat up above the high tide mark. Then, armed with swords, battleaxes and round, patterned shields, they set off, striding up the dunes not twenty metres away and down the other side, while Troy sat dumbstruck. He looked around for cameras, but there were none. Not a film, then. Even the dog-walker had gone. Some university department doing a reconstruction? Maybe.

Troy got to his feet and, brushing the worst of the damp sand from his jeans as he went, set off after the men. He took long strides on the downward slope in his haste not to lose them, digging in his heels to keep himself from falling headlong, ignoring the cold sand spilling into his shoes. Instead of following the track down to the road, the men had chosen a footpath that snaked among clumps of bushes. One moment they were there walking in single file, then gone, to reappear much further on than he expected, and off to the right, where the path was barely visible. He thought he'd lost them altogether, then there they were, tramping across the first of the fields, bunched up again in twos and threes, the helmsman at their head.

Troy struggled through a thicket because that was where the path seemed to lead, though it would have been quicker to have found a way round. Scrambled over a stile into the field. Where were they? In the time they'd been out of his sight, he didn't think they would have made it to the gate on the other side, but there was no other way they could have gone. Though his legs were aching and he had a stitch in his side, Troy set off again across the field.

Slowly, slowly he became aware of something – not someone – behind him, shadowing his footsteps. At first it was no more than a whisper of movement in the air. Then a vibration through the soles of his shoes. A presence, coming closer, growing more real with every step. As if the beast, too, had tracked him from out of his dream. Grendel! Fear rose up through him, lifting the hackles on his neck.

He stopped. Nothing. Imagination – no! There *was* something there. He could feel the warmth of it in the air, like hot breath on his back.

He took a few steps more. Again came that faintest trembling of the earth under his feet.

'*Face your fear!*'

Who said that?

No one.

Which was worse? Knowing what was there? Or not knowing? Troy swung round.

A group of maybe two dozen cows stood watching him. Young ones, heifers, curious to know what he was doing in their field.

Spooked by a bunch of cows? *Get a grip!* he told himself. *Walk on.*

The heifers were following him. He knew it, even before he turned to look and found they'd closed the gap by several metres. At the same time they'd spread out into a curved line, closing off any chance of escape.

He walked backwards a few steps. The cows didn't move. But as soon as he turned away he could sense the shuffle of interest behind him.

Just keep walking, they won't hurt you. But his legs were so tired. He stumbled once, recovered quickly, but not before he'd heard a short, sharp galloping of hooves. What if he tripped now and fell? They'd be all over him in a minute.

He turned again. The cows stood still. He shouted at them, 'Go away! Get back!'

And heard an answering shout from the gate at the edge of the field behind him, 'Stay where you are! Don't move!'

Out of the corner of his eye he saw a black and white dog streak into view, barking, bouncing, feinting, taking them on. The cows suddenly not sure of themselves, whether they were supposed to chase the dog or be chased by it. The dog gave a sharp bark and made a rush towards the cow nearest Troy, which waited till the dog was right up close, then frisked away. The dog let it go and homed in on another.

The voice behind him came again. 'Come on then! Walk! Don't run.'

Run? You've got to be joking. Troy turned and stumbled the rest of the way to the gate, hauled himself over it, and hung on till his legs felt fit again to hold him upright. 'Thanks,' he said.

'That's OK.' She was a girl about his age, maybe a year or so older. Maybe not. It was hard to tell with girls. Fleece, jeans and serious hiking boots. Nice hair, short and shiny, conker-brown. 'My mum says there ought to be a sign up,' she said, 'to warn people about those cows.'

Troy leaned on the gate, forcing himself to breathe deep, massaging the stitch in his side. 'They're just heifers – young ones. They're not really dangerous, just a bit playful, that's all.'

'Tell that to the old lady they put in the hospital last week.'

The dog was back by her feet, tongue hanging out, waiting for a word of praise. It didn't get one.

The girl snapped the lead back on to its collar. 'Lucky I had the dog with me for a decoy.'

'Weren't you worried he might get hurt?'

'Dogs can take care of themselves. Anyway, if it really was the dog or you, what would you do?'

There was no answer to that.

She started walking away down the footpath that led back towards the village, leaving him – expecting him? – to follow. 'I'm Zoe, by the way,' she tossed over her shoulder. 'Zoe Jenkins.'

'Hi, Zoe. I'm—'

'Troy Sheridan. I know. You're staying with that funny old couple at the post office.'

'Dad calls me Tel. Short for Terry.' Why was he telling her that? Like she cared.

'What's his name, then?' Troy called after her.

'Who?'

'Him. The dog.'

'Oh! Rusty. Don't ask me why. Ask my dad.'

Troy broke into a trot so he could catch her up. 'My dad says I can have a dog, once we're settled. He's coming to fetch me soon. My dad.'

Zoe stopped dead, pulling Rusty up short on his hind legs as she swung to face Troy, mouth open, ready to say she knew better than he did. But all she said in the end was, 'Yes. Right.' She turned away again, walking on. 'What were you doing in that field anyway?' she asked.

Then he remembered. 'I was following *them*!'

'Them?' She peered at him over her shoulder, frowning. 'Who's them?'

'That bunch of men dressed up as Vikings. They must have come right past you.'

'No.'

'Was it you I saw down on the beach? With the dog? You *must* have seen them then. They had this boat. I thought at first they were making a film, then maybe one of those historical reconstruction thingies . . .'

They stopped at a fork in the path, where it curved either way round the glorified hummock known locally as Drake's Hill. The rest of the country round was so flat that from the top of it you could see for miles. He and Dad used to race one another up the side. First thing they always did when they got here, never mind the weather.

Zoe was staring at him, shaking her head. 'I didn't see any Vikings. There was no boat. There was just me and Rusty down on the beach, and you perched like a pixie on top of the dunes. Heel!' she snapped, with an angry little tug on the lead, dragging the dog away from a drift of dead leaves. 'I go this way.' She pointed. 'That way'll take you back to the shop.'

'I *know* that!' Troy muttered, as she walked away without so much as 'See you around.' 'Bye, Rusty.' The dog looked back wistfully over its shoulder. If Zoe's dad wanted his dog walking, Troy wouldn't mind doing it. He'd make a heckuvva better job of it than she did.

She did have nice hair, though.

She was winding him up, that's all, pretending not to have seen what she *must* have seen if she wasn't walking about with her eyes shut. Girls liked to do that, swear black was white when it suited them, just to wrong-foot you.

Four

He let himself in through the shop, expecting to find customers from the black 4 × 4 parked out front, and Flo busy behind the counter. But there was only Mrs Belcher, clutching a brown paper parcel with enough string looped round it to make a fair-sized fishing net. Mrs Belcher expected parcels to come undone in the post. Hers usually did.

'Troy!' she exclaimed.

'Hallo, Mrs Belcher.'

'No Doris today?'

'She's gone to the hospital. With her leg. I'll tell Flo you're here, shall I?'

'I think they've got company.' With the air of an early Christian martyr on being told the lions would be a little late today, 'I can wait,' she said.

'I'll tell her anyway.' Troy pushed open the door to the house.

'I was sorry to hear about your – your sad loss.'

'Yes. Thanks.'

'But we should count our blessings.'

As the door swung to behind him, Troy wondered vaguely what she meant.

There was no one in the kitchen. No one in the living room on the other side of the passage. The voices seemed to be coming from the cold little parlour beyond, where the heating from the Aga never reached. He caught his own name, 'Troy,' spoken by a voice he didn't recognize. The 'company' Mrs Belcher mentioned? Owner of the 4 × 4?

Then Stan: 'How much should we tell him?'

About what? Troy wondered.

'Nothing,' said the stranger.

Stan again: 'Nothing? What if he asks questions?'

Troy edged closer. There wasn't much to see through the crack where the door had been left ajar. The backs of Stan's and Flo's heads, sitting side by side on the chintz settee. The stranger, soft-spoken, still invisible. 'You must be very careful how you answer them.'

'I won't lie to him,' said Stan.

'If you're not sure you can cope with this, there are places . . . experts . . .'

'We wouldn't dream of it!' Stan stopped him quietly, but firm as a rock.

Then came Flo's voice: 'I thought everyone agreed this would be the best place for him, for the time being. Till his mum's got herself settled.'

Troy frowned, puzzled; what had Mum got to do with it?

'It's not going to be easy,' said the invisible man.

Stan's voice again: 'We've coped with all kinds. Haven't we, Flo? Never given up on a child yet.'

30

Then Flo: 'I remember when his dad first came to us . . .'

'He used to set fire to things,' said Stan, a smile in his voice, remembering.

'I had to hide all the matches . . . firelighters . . . paraffin . . . But Stan took him all round lighting bonfires for people . . .'

'He was afraid of fire,' Stan said softly. (Dad afraid of fire? He never knew that.) 'We never knew why. He just had to learn to face his fear. After that, he was as right as ninepence.'

'Never any trouble. Two or three times a year he used to come. His mum used to phone us – just pick up the phone, we said—'

'And I'd go and fetch him.'

'He was like a son to us. Having Troy here . . .' Her voice died away.

Then came a silence. Troy pushed the door open.

Three startled faces turned towards him. Flo, Stan, and the old man sitting in the comfy chair beside the electric fire. There was a faint whiff of scorching from his corduroy trousers. Flo's face was flushed from the fire and her eyes were watering. She dabbed at them with her hankie and blew her nose. Nobody spoke.

'I went for a walk,' said Troy, breaking the silence. 'Down through the village.'

'How was it?' asked Stan.

'Oh, you know. Much the same.'

'This is Dr Munro,' said Flo. She busied herself collecting up the teacups. 'You remember Dr Munro, Troy. From when you had the earache?' She added the sugar bowl to the tray. 'He's just popped in to take a look at you.'

'Dr Munro?' Troy took a step back. What was this? Dr Munro was thirty-something with mousy hair and a ginger moustache, and smelt of garlic and peppermints. He shook his head: 'No.'

Flo gave him an odd look. 'It's all right, Troy.' She turned to the stranger. 'I think he's had his fill of doctors for a bit.'

The old man smiled, thin lips parting over crooked teeth. 'I understand. That's why we thought it would be better if I examined you here, Troy, rather than down at the surgery.'

'He's just come to take a look at you.'

Looking was what he was doing, with his watery grey eyes. Let him look all he wanted. Stare straight back. That always fazes them.

Then Stan said, 'This is Dr Munro senior, Troy, who used to have the practice. I think it was young Dr Munro that Troy saw, Flo.'

'Was it?' Flo said absently, knocking over a cup, slopping cold tea on to the biscuits. 'I must have been thinking of . . . some other time. Is it really that long since you retired, John?'

The old man nodded. 'I'm afraid your average GP doesn't have much time for house calls nowadays, Troy. So I give my son a hand when I can.'

32

'I almost forgot,' said Troy, still staring the old man out. 'Mrs Belcher's waiting in the shop. She's got a parcel to post.'

Flo said, 'I'd better go and see to her. We'll leave you two to it. Can you bring the biscuits, Stan?'

It just seemed to be the usual MOT. He'd had plenty of those in the hospital. Temperature, blood pressure, reflexes, eyes, ears, throat, chest. 'Sorry if my hands are cold.' The doctor's hands weren't cold, but soft and clingy as cobwebs. 'Still taking the tablets?'

'Yes.' When he remembered; though he did his best to forget. They messed with his brain and stole away his dreams.

'Good lad. Let's have a look at that scar, hm?' He pushed back the hair from Troy's forehead. 'It's healed up nicely. Hm. A nice neat job.' Finally he sat back. 'Any problems?'

Troy shook his head.

'Headaches? Nightmares?'

'No.'

'Hm! And what's the last thing you remember?'

Troy fingered the scar. 'Before the hospital, you mean?'

The doctor nodded.

Troy frowned. It was always the same, each time he tried to think back, as if when they sliced his head open they'd taken part of his brain away. Part of his memories. 'I remember . . . I remember, as I went out, Mum called to me, not to forget my coat.'

The doctor nodded gravely.

Troy had a picture in his mind now. Mum hopping from foot to bare foot on the doorstep, the coat in her hand; himself halfway down the drive. He had to go back and take it off her. As he got into the car he let the coat, with its designer label, slip to the pavement, one sleeve trailing in a puddle.

Dad, as he drove off, was grinning ear to ear. 'Think you might have dropped something there, Tel. Bit of old duvet, it looked like.'

'Donald bought it. I don't want it.'

'You need a new coat? I'll buy you a coat. Any sort of coat you want.' He brandished a fistful of notes. 'Got a hot tip for the big race yesterday, from a stable lad I did a favour for six months back. Rank outsider. Down to six-to-four by the time they came under starter's orders. And he strolled home! Pure magic! Nice day out, too. I could take you next year.'

'You know Mum'd never let me.'

'I know.'

Each time Dad sat in the car outside waiting, he never once turned round to look at her, not that Troy ever saw. Only sometimes, a couple of miles down the road, he'd suddenly say something like, 'She's had her hair done different.'

'Yes.'

'Do you think it suits her?'

'I don't know. What do you think?'

'I think I liked her better the way she looked before. Didn't you?'

Troy didn't tell the doctor any of that. Just Mum calling out to him, not to forget his coat.

'And did you?'

'Did I what?'

'Forget it. Or take it?'

'Yes. No. I don't know.'

'Hm! Never mind.' The old man looked at him with sad, misty eyes. 'The memories will come back. In their own time. We must be patient.'

'Can I go now?'

'Eh? Yes, yes, of course.'

He found Flo in the kitchen, making a major operation out of clearing away the tea things.

'Finished already, Troy? That's good.' She bustled a bit more, transferring the leftover biscuits that were savable to their tin, taking the tin to the cupboard, then coming back for the sugar basin. She picked up the stacked crockery from the table and carried it the three steps to the draining board, which was as far as she could go with Stan stood at the sink, stolidly mixing paint in an old ice-cream carton.

'Well!' she said tightly, 'I suppose I'd better go and show the doctor out.'

Troy caught a burst of murmured words as the parlour door opened, before it closed behind her.

Talking about him. What was it they weren't supposed to tell him? He thought of asking Stan. But Stan still stood with his back turned, working away, though the paint must be well mixed by now.

So Troy walked through to the shop. No customers. Which was good. He ran his hand over the polished wood counter, drinking in the mingled scents of apples and cheese and mothballs and candles, spiced with the dust of home-grown veg wafting through from the lean-to at the back; feeling the unevenness of the rough wooden boards under his feet; scanning the shelves crammed to bursting with knitting wool, plimsolls, birthday cards, paper clips, rubber bands and biros; shoelaces, shoe polish, shampoo and hairslides. Everything in its place. Good. Groceries this side, cereals and sugar, tea and coffee, tins of baked beans, dog food, processed peas and soup. Name an item and he could find it blindfold.

Summer visitors, stopping on impulse for a packet of cigarettes or a bag of crisps, barely used to smother their giggles till they got outside: 'You'll never believe it! It's like something out of Miss Marple or *Dad's Army*! You go in! Go on, go see for yourself!' So what? What supermarket would sell you toilet rolls one at a time, or just two eggs, or slice bacon to the exact thickness you wanted, never mind deliver a box of groceries at no extra charge? Flo provided a service and she was proud of it.

After the first lull there was a fairly steady stream of customers today. Nearly all of them Troy knew by name, the rest by sight. How was he? they kept asking. He was fine, thanks. What else do you say?

No one wanting ham off the bone or anything from the post office, so he didn't need to call for Flo. A pound of carrots and one onion he could cope with; a pack of rubber bands; a tin of mushroom soup; a birthday card ready for sending at the end of November – 'If I don't buy it now, I know I'll forget. And how are you, Troy?'

'I'm fine. Did you want a stamp?'

'No! No. Plenty of time for that.'

Odd, the things people seemed to have run out of today and couldn't manage without. They kept looking at him in a funny way. *OK, I've been in hospital, but I haven't grown an extra ear or anything, so will you please stop staring at me!*

Captain Peasgrove, off on his daily litter patrol of the local footpaths, but dressed, as usual, for an attempt on the north face of the Eiger, came in to collect the packed lunch Flo had put ready. 'Ah, Troy! Good man. Glad to see you keeping busy, much the best thing. We must soldier on. Soldier on!'

Little Miss Moffatt gathered her modest groceries into a handknitted string bag, then splashed out on a family-size bar of fruit and nut, which she shyly pushed back over the counter. 'That's for you,' she murmured. 'Poor boy!' And scuttled out.

Troy stood with the bar of chocolate in his hand. He knew if he ate it the chocolate would have about as much taste as the paper round it. So he put the package back on the display, pressed No Sale, and took the price of it out of the till in ten- and twenty-pence pieces, useful for phone calls. Dad had been a bit remiss on the pocket-money front, as usual.

As he slammed the till-drawer back in place, slipping the money into his pocket, he turned to see her watching him from the other side of the counter. Her. The girl. What was her name? Zoe. Zoe Jenkins. He hadn't heard the bell. She must have slipped in as Miss Moffatt left. Been watching him all this time.

'I wasn't nicking it,' he said. 'The money. I just changed my mind, that's all, about the chocolate. I was just taking my money out again.'

She nodded. 'If you say so.' The tilt of her head said, Why should I care? Either way? 'Two hundred grams of dairy toffees, please.'

'Two hundred grams?' Troy reached the jar down from the shelf and began tipping the sweets on to the scales. Flo had bought a set of metric weights, because The Law said she must – but most of her customers still liked to see the stuff they were buying weighed out in old money. He ought to know what two hundred grams looked like, but he didn't. One kilo is two pounds two ounces, give or take, so two hundred grams is less than a quarter of that, which would be just under half a pound. Or should that be over? he wondered, as the scale pan went on filling up without a sign of dipping to balance the weights he'd put on the other side.

It didn't help to have Zoe watching, though every time he looked up her glance slid away to somewhere just beyond his shoulder.

Still the foil-wrapped sweets kept piling up and the scales showed no sign of dipping. 'I don't know what's wrong with them!' he said. 'That must be two hundred grams, don't you think?'

She answered, sphinx-like, 'You tell me.'

He had to fetch one of the brown vegetable bags, because none of the white ones was big enough. Troy started shovelling the toffees in. 'Are you sure that's enough?'

'Maybe just a couple more.' Eyes focussed somewhere over his shoulder again. Then suddenly, 'OK, that'll do.' She grabbed the bag, slammed some coins down on the counter and left, leaving the shop bell jangling behind her as Flo came in from the kitchen.

'She wants watching, that one,' Flo observed.

Troy hastily counted the money in his hand, rang up the same amount on the till and chucked it in.

'What did she want anyway?' asked Flo.

'Just some sweets.'

Flo shifted the Save the Children box, which had got itself wedged underneath the pan of the scales, preventing it from dipping. 'All right, Troy. Thanks for helping out. I'll take over now. Stan wants a word with you, out the back.'

'What about?'

'He didn't say.'

'Is it the surprise? You said this morning he'd got a surprise for me.'

She winked. 'Off you go now.'

Hating Zoe Jenkins – who was she, anyway? She didn't belong in Elm Green; not the Elm Green he knew – Troy made his way through to the back.

Five

Outside the back door, Stan was wiping his hands on a bit of old pillowcase. The little pine cupboard stood beside him, minus its doors, but wearing a fine new coat of white woodwash which let the grain of the wood show through. 'Not bad,' Stan decided. 'Not bad for a little old cupboard I picked up at the car boot for two pound. Eh, Troy?'

Troy nodded. 'It's looking good.'

'You know what that old skinflint Leakey was offering? Fifty p! I couldn't let him get away with that. Fifty p would have been an insult to the man that made it. Fifty p – and a fifty pound price tag the minute Leakey puts it in his shop, without so much as running a duster over it!' Stan spread the bit of pillowcase on the sunward side of a rosemary bush to dry. He began rolling himself a cigarette. 'Did you go far this morning?'

'Just down through the village, as far as the sea.'

'Making sure it was all still there?'

'Something like that.'

Stan ran his tongue along the edge of the cigarette paper, sealed it, and felt for his matches. No mention yet of the surprise. There was never any point in trying to hurry Stan. Stan would get around to saying what was on his mind in his own good time. 'You didn't come back by Peppercorn Lane?'

'No.'

'There's some new people moved in to Mrs Rainbird's old place.'

'Oh?' said Troy.

Stan nodded, drew on his cigarette. 'Name of Jenkins. Retired schoolteacher and his wife. She's manageress of the charity shop in Seahaven. Seen him a couple of times in the pub. They've got a girl about your age.'

Zoe Jenkins. Right! From Drake's Hill, the path she took would have brought her out near the end of Peppercorn Lane. 'Have they got a dog?' Troy asked.

Stan gave him a quizzical look. 'Border collie mostly, by the look of him. You still prefer dogs to girls?'

'I saw a girl with a dog down on the beach. That's all.' Troy swiftly moved on: 'There was a bunch of heifers in the far field, up by the dunes.'

Stan smiled. 'Lively creatures. Surprised you, did they?'

Troy shrugged. 'Didn't even notice them till I was halfway across. Is it right they put an old lady in the hospital?'

'Oh? Who told you that?'

'Just someone who came in the shop.'

'Friend of Miss Moffatt's, down from town for the weekend. Not used to livestock. She lost her cool and tried to run for it. Tripped and fell and broke her wrist. That's all. Cows never touched her.'

'I thought it was probably something like that.'

'Miss Moffatt was most upset. Like it was her fault. Best not to mention it.'

'Right.'

'That's about it. Sum total of all the gossip since you were last here. You might check with Doris tomorrow, see if I've missed anything, but I doubt it.'

Troy nodded sagely, like a true-born countryman. The sort of nod that cuts out the need for further conversation. After that there was silence for a bit. No problem. Stan's silences were more comfortable to live with than other people's small talk. 'Oh, by the way ...' Stan pinched out his roll-up and thriftily tucked it behind his ear for later. He ducked into the shed and came back pushing an elderly, but spotlessly clean and freshly-oiled, boys' bike. 'What do you think?'

Was this the surprise? Troy wasn't sure what to say. He looked the bike over. It wasn't what you'd call state-of-the-art. Still wondering, he wandered round and looked at it from the other side. Hours Stan must have spent, taking it apart, cleaning each piece, then putting it all back together.

Stan watched him. 'Better than walking, any road, eh?'

'Where did you get it?'

'It was your dad's,' Stan said fondly. 'I've had it tucked away for I don't know how long, always meaning to get it cleaned up, but you know how it is.'

42

Troy knew. The back of the shed was crammed with odds and ends that Stan was convinced only needed a bit of tender loving care. But first there was the gardening to do and all the fetching and carrying for the shop, since Flo had never learned to drive. Then someone would ask him to take a quick look at a lawnmower that wouldn't start; or there'd be some old lady who couldn't afford to get a man in to decorate.

'So, what do you think, Troy? Will it do you?'

'It'll do.' Dad's old bike. 'It's great, Stan. Thanks.'

'Can we just check I've got the height of the saddle right? Then, soon as we've had a spot of lunch, you can take it out and road-test it.'

Lunch was ham from Flo's tame pork butcher down the road in Ashfield, who still did his own slaughtering, curing and sausage-making. Salad, fresh from the garden and greenhouse. Sweet lettuce, sun-ripe tomatoes, crisp radishes and succulent, purple beetroot.

But after a mouthful or two the food lost its flavour and Troy sat forking it round his plate till Flo was called away to the shop again. He pushed the bunny-food into a heap, trying to make it look as if he'd eaten at least half, and said to Stan, 'Can I go now? Try out that bike?'

Stan nodded, hooked out the biggest piece of the ham from underneath the lettuce on Troy's plate and transferred it to his own. 'Just take it gently, eh? Don't overdo it. Or Flo'll have my guts for fiddlestrings.'

He pushed the bike out into the lane and made sure it was pointing in the right direction before he got on. It was a long time since he'd ridden a bike. Take it easy, Stan said, but the faster you go on a bike, the easier it gets. Easy as falling off a log – whoops! nearly came off there, taking that bend too fast, sliding on a patch of gravel. Stan was right about it being better than walking. With a bike he could go further and faster, on down the lane, turning right at the Green away from the route he'd taken that morning, narrowly missing two old ladies unloading their supermarket shopping from the bus. Past the church and Parson's Spinney. Outside The New Inn, a couple of old-timers enjoying the autumn sunshine were left standing with their pint pots halfway to their mouths, wondering whether they hadn't tumbled back in time some twenty years. Or was it no more than a ghost they were seeing? Same bike, similar boy flying past. Same floppy fair hair, same pointed chin.

With the ghost of the boy his dad once was for company Troy pedalled on, the wind in his hair and the cold air slapping his cheeks, heading uphill towards the main road and the cycle path running parallel.

The blare of a juggernaut's horn nearly knocked him out of the saddle. Like he was the sort of lamebrain who was going to cycle straight out in front! 'Road hog!' he yelled after it and wished he'd kept his mouth shut as the dust whipped at his tongue and his throat caught the acrid taste of diesel. Then his legs gave way. He felt sick and giddy – and stupid. Stupid! He crouched by the roadside, waiting for the weakness to pass, while cars, vans and lorries rushed by, unseeing, uncaring.

'And you a boy of no account that I found crying by the roadside.' The blind man's words re-echoed inside his head. No! That was in another place, a different world . . .

Troy brushed the tears of frustration away. Stan had warned him against overdoing it, but he hadn't come that far!

Still feeling wobbly, glad of the bike to lean on, he pulled himself up and pushed it the odd hundred metres – seemed more like a mile! – to the turning that led back down into the village. He cocked his leg over the saddle and scooted along till he got up enough speed to freewheel, turned left into Peppercorn Lane and stopped again outside the house he would always think of as Mrs Rainbird's. He'd left it till last on purpose. Incomers sometimes did terrible things – like buying places just so they could knock them down and put up a smart, modern bungalow.

The beehives were long gone, of course. And the house martins' nests from under the eaves. But the thatch still tipped rakishly over the left-hand bedroom window, the paint was still peeling from the windowsills and it was only the honeysuckle and ivy which kept the plaster pinned to the walls. Troy

45

breathed a sigh of relief. He half expected to see Mrs Rainbird come trotting round the corner dressed in her widow's black and cherry-red Doc Martens. Mrs Rainbird, bright and quick, fit enough to dance the hokey-cokey at her ninetieth-birthday bash. Mrs Rainbird, confiding to him after her fifth double port and lemon that she never reckoned the weather had turned really cold till the po under her bed froze over, and never a day's illness in her life.

Mrs Rainbird fell off a roof the following June, trying to round up a maverick swarm of bees, broke her hip and died of a virus she picked up in the hospital. Strange to think he'd never, ever see her again. He'd never known anyone who'd died before.

'Man's life is brief,' the blind man said, *'as the flight of a swallow through the mead-hall by night. From the darkness he comes; to the darkness he returns.'*

Evening shadows gathered round Troy. There was a tang of woodsmoke in the air. Someone must be having a bonfire.

Then his ears caught the trembling notes of the harp. He began to make out a murmur of voices.

'How many did the old man say he killed?'

'Who? Grendel? Thirty, at the last count.'

Thirty lives snuffed out. But the world kept turning.

Slowly, seamlessly, the easy-going warmth of the mead-hall folded itself around him, its patterns of flickering light and hazy darkness, its cooking smells and scents of woodsmoke, candle grease, leather and sheepskin, dogs and unwashed bodies.

'Thirty, eh? Hic!'

'Belts, buckles and all.'

'Belts, buckles and boots. Don't forget the boots.'

'A nice touch, that.'

'Bit indigestible, I would have thought. Hic!'

Through the smoky half-light, Troy glimpsed the ruin of once-proud Heorot, dead leaves scattered and eddying across the dusty floor; the tapestries torn and spattered with blood; broken sticks of furniture, festooned with cobwebs, piled up like scrapwood against the walls. The place was the mead-hall. And it was Heorot. Neither quite one nor the other, but somehow, through the blind man's magic, both together.

'Owl pellets!' the man on his left barked suddenly.

'What?'

'Belts, buckles and whatnot. He spits 'em all out again like owl pellets.'

'You reckon?'

'Have you got a better idea? Hey-up! We're off again.'

Softly, the blind man's lilting voice drew the listeners back into the story.

'In the harrowed hall of Heorot, the King received the fifteen strangers. Tall, young and fair they were, and the battle-light was in their eyes. And the brightest and the best of them was Beowulf!'

Troy's heart gave a lurch of excitement, not surprise, as he took in the face . . . the smile . . . the long, fair hair . . . the way the man stood – everything about him! It was the steersman from the ship he'd seen that morning. The little ship that seemed to skim like a seabird, above the waves not on them. A slowly-building roar of 'Beowulf!' echoed round the table behind him, mead-cups drumming on the wooden boards.

'Picture Hrothgar,' the blind man murmured, drawing his audience back again, 'the haunted King, his hair now grizzled grey, his face furrowed by long, sleepless nights, his swordsmen slain, or sailed away to serve a king not cursed. Yet the sight of the hero brings a smile to his lips.

' "Beowulf!" He turns to the faithful few that serve him still. "You remember Egtheow? My old friend, Egtheow? This is Beowulf, Egtheow's son. Beowulf Egtheowsson! What brings you to Heorot?"

' "Grendel!" ' The name rang out like a challenge. A young man's voice in an old blind man's mouth.

Then he was Hrothgar again, world-weary. 'No.' The word hardly more than a sigh.

' "You think you can kill Grendel?" Sadly Hrothgar shook his head. "Beowulf, for twelve, long years men like you have come, more than I can remember, greedy for glory, and left not even their names behind them. Not a scrap to burn or bury. Over the wasteland their sad souls wander, still searching for Grendel, still without the power to harm him. There is a charm laid on the monster by the hell-hag that spawned him. No axe or spear or sword can wound him."

' "So I'll face him without axe or spear or sword!"

' "The monster has the strength of thirty men!"

' "In this right arm," said Beowulf, "I have the strength of thirty men and more. All those brave men Grendel has killed will lend their strength to mine. Their blood cries out for blood. Grendel's life for theirs."

'And Hrothgar answered, half daring to dream at last of an end to the nightmare, "What if he kills you too?"

'Beowulf smiled. "No man lives for ever. If it is my fate to die tonight, I'd rather die with my eyes wide open, fighting this monster face to face, hand to hand, than safe asleep and in my bed. So let's tell the world King Hrothgar feasts in his own hall again tonight!"

'The King bowed his head. "Make it so!" '

'Amen . . .' 'Yes . . .' 'Make it so!' 'Let be what will be.' The whispers ran round the table. That was the way for men to live – or die!

The bard's voice ran on: 'In Heorot the benches and tables were dragged out and dusted down, those broken beyond repair tossed aside for firewood, the rest patched up and set in place. Tapestries were shaken, brushed and rehung, draped to hide the worst of the damage.'

Faster and faster the harp music ran and leapt and

danced. Troy watched as the last cobwebs were brushed away, and the dead leaves and bird droppings. Fires were lit, the men of Heorot took their places and the feast was carried in.

'Oh, savour the smell of it!' the blind man cried. 'Taste the ripe flesh of venison, boar, mutton, wildfowl and eels; the fragrant sauces scented with garlic, parsley, sage, rosemary and thyme; and the fresh-baked bread, piled high.

'As the mead-cup was passed around, amid the talk and the songs and the laughter, it seemed quite like the old times. But then – oh, then! – as the sun slid to his rest, and the torches were kindled, Hrothgar's men remembered Grendel. One by one they slipped away. Drowsy darkness spread over the sleeping land, and there was no soul left in Heorot but Beowulf and his fourteen followers, still picking over the bones, still supping one more sip of mead, or singing one more song. It had been a cold, hard journey, even in summer weather. Heorot was warm and comfortable. Grendel would not come yet . . .'

One by one the men settled themselves to sleep till there was no one left awake but Troy, the watcher, moving silently between the tables, circling round the sleepers. He felt braver this time, with Beowulf there.

But what if, when the monster came, the hero didn't wake in time?

What if the beast was there already, shrouded in shadow, outside the hall? He strained his ears for the faintest footfall, the whispering that was not the wind.

The doors hung useless, half off their hinges. There'd be no warning crash this time.

One by one the flickering torches died. He stirred the fires, so as to give a little light. Someone had to stay on watch. Time passed, and Grendel did not come. Time passed, or else stood still, no ticking of the clock to mark it. Troy felt his eyelids begin to droop, then jerked awake with a sudden rush of terror. The certain knowledge that the beast was there, in the pitch darkness outside. The air was too still. Not a breath of night wind through the open door. There was something in the way. Something huge. Something that moved. The faintest vibration travelling through the ground under his feet.

Troy froze. He opened his mouth to shout a warning, but gagged on a stench of marsh gas, slime, and carrion. Watched, helpless, as a scaly arm slid through the open door to seize the nearest sleeper. In two bites, the man was gone. Grendel licked the blood from off his warty lips and cast about for his next victim.

'If it is my fate to die tonight . . .' Troy muttered to himself, trying to believe it, because it was what Beowulf believed. But let it be someone else! He couldn't move a muscle. Couldn't breathe. And the scent of his terror drew the monster to him. One huge, taloned hand swooped down—

Troy felt himself whisked backwards, tumbling head over heels, scaly talons scraping past his cheek.

Beowulf was bending over him, eyes wide with surprise, running a hand through his long blond hair. 'You?' he said. 'What are you doing here?'

Troy, staring over the hero's shoulder, saw the mailed fist sweep down again. 'Behind you!' he yelled.

In a single movement, Beowulf thrust the boy under a table out of harm's way and swung round to meet the blow. Instead of dodging it, he rode it, fastening on the monster's arm.

The beast let out a roar of fury, and – yes! – fear.

The mead-hall was filled with the sound of tankards drumming, voices yelling: 'Hold him!' 'Hang on!' 'Be-o-wulf!' While in Heorot Beowulf's grip held fast, legs braced, riding the threshing and bucking of the monster, like steering a ship across a storm-tossed sea.

Tables and benches and men, too, went flying. Hangings were ripped from the walls.

'Kill the beast!' the voices roared. 'Kill the beast!' 'Kill!' 'Kill!' 'Kill!'

The talons of Grendel's free hand were gouging deep scratches down the pillars, tearing the doors clean off their hinges. Blood bubbled from the monster's scaly shoulder as the skin began to split. Still Beowulf had him fast.

Maddened by pain and terror, the shrieking beast pulled harder. Until skin, sinews, tendons, stretched till they could stretch no more, burst apart.

Howling, howling, howling, Grendel fled into the night, his lifeblood dripping from his shoulder, leaving his loathsome arm gripped fast by Beowulf.

Troy crawled shakily out from under the table. He felt like an old, used dishcloth, all the energy wrung out of him. But good. Really good! It was over! The enemy that stalked his dreams was as good as dead, and he was watching that massive arm being nailed up – knock, knock, knock! – for the world to see and wonder at.

The noise of celebration spilled out into the night. Women and children came running to join the men crowding round the hero. Fires were rekindled, the mead flowed again, and the leftovers from the night before were hastily reheated, though outside the dawn was already breaking.

And whether this was the King's own mead-hall, or the fabled hall of Heorot, who was to say?

Only the blind bard, sitting lost in thought while the blizzard of sound and movement raged around him.

Troy blinked and when he looked again there were not so many of them as there had been before.

He rubbed his eyes, and there were fewer still. Like guests quietly slipping away so as not to spoil the party, till there was only the blind man sitting alone, a faint smile playing about his lips, as if he knew something they did not, and the rest were no more than shadows.

Then, in the blink of an eye, he, too, was gone.

It was morning and Troy was lying in his own room, with no memory at all of how he'd got himself home the night before, or what he'd had for supper, or done to fill in the hours till bedtime. Only that Beowulf had saved him and Grendel was dead.

Six

It had rained hard during the night. The wind had shredded the clouds to tatters and spread them out to dry against a watery-blue sky. Gulls pitched and tossed like flecks of white seafoam. Troy flung open the window. The cold caught his breath for a moment, but the air was gloriously bright and clear, spiced with the salty tang of the sea.

Grendel was dead.

Grendel's dead! He wanted to shout the news for all the world to hear, but he knew that would only lead to awkward questions.

He could see the tail of the bike, safely stowed under cover of Stan's workshed. So that was OK. Somehow he'd got himself home last night.

He clattered downstairs – *Have you cleaned your teeth, Troy?* I think so. *Taken your tablets?* Can't remember, two minutes ago and he truly couldn't say for sure – but the pieces of last evening were beginning to fall into place. Rain pattering outside the window. Radio playing in the background, a mixture of music and talk. Flo knitting her 'Teddies for Tragedies', clickety-clack, clickety-clack, faster and faster, like she was going for *The Guinness Book of Records*. Hundreds of them she must have made over the years, each with its own little drawstring bag, and packed them off to Mozambique, Kosovo, Bangladesh, Afghanistan, to little kids who'd lost everything, so as to give them something to love and look after.

Stan and himself playing cribbage, scoring fifteen-two, fifteen-four.

Usually Troy loved to play cards. Dad had taught him well. Tonight his mind wasn't on it, running on autopilot. He kept making stupid mistakes, till Stan plucked two of the matches from the scoreboard and, smiling, offered them to him, to keep his eyes propped open. 'Why don't you go to bed, Troy?' he suggested quietly, like it was no big deal, no brownie points to be earned by sticking it out till grown-up bedtime.

But then at the same time he seemed to be in the mead-hall . . . Could you be in two places – two worlds – at once? Two separate worlds; like the mead-hall and Heorot – separate, yet part of one another? It was a puzzle.

There was no breakfast laid for him in the kitchen this morning. Flo, turning from the sink, said, 'I thought it best to wait till you came down. Just cereal's fine, if that's all you want.' Still wishing he'd ask for something more.

Troy, wanting to please her, share the good feeling he'd got about this morning, considered a moment, then said, 'Have you got Ready Brek?' He thought he might just manage that.

'Of course I've got Ready Brek!' She set a pan of milk on to heat and bustled through to the shop, leaving the door propped open. He could hear Doris serving a customer: '. . . Jaffa Cakes, eight fondant fancies: you must be expecting visitors this weekend, Mrs Belcher. And a variety pack of cereals. Theresa and the twins, is it? That reminds me, we've got this new stuff in, very good for getting stains out of carpets . . .' The door swung shut, cutting her off in mid-flow, then opened again almost at once. '. . . Yes, we have got garibaldis: on the other hand there's gingernuts on offer this week, fifteen pence off, that's quite a saving . . .'

Flo entered at the double, opening the cereal packet on the fly. 'What's the betting,' she chuckled, 'she ends up buying both? Eh, Troy? She's wasted here, is our Doris; she ought to be working for one of those big multinationals.' She whisked the milkpan off the hob just as it was bubbling up. 'Syrup or jam?'

'Is it strawberry?'

'Stan's home-made.'

'Well, then. No contest.'

He spooned jam on to his hot Ready Brek and stirred it round. It tasted good. But it was hard work getting it down with Flo watching every mouthful while she pretended to be busy at the sink. He put down his spoon. 'Sorry, I can't manage any more.'

'Never mind. You did your best. My fault for giving you too much.'

Oh, shut up, Flo! It is not your fault! He got up quickly and went to the shop door, brushing the sudden rush of tears away.

He could feel Flo's anxious eyes following him. 'Still, better too much than too little!' she exclaimed brightly, gathering up the dish and spoon.

In the shop, Mrs Belcher, with her hands folded across her middle and a look like she'd just seen what the cat dragged in, watched Doris totting up. '. . . seven, plus nine, plus eight,' muttered Doris, 'call that three eights. Twenty-four. Plus nine, is thirty-th . . .'

He'd tried to explain to her once how the till would add up the prices for her and work out the change. 'So I end up with a brain all withered like a walnut from lack of use?' she exclaimed. 'No, thank you!'

'Hallo,' said Troy.

'Troy!' beamed Doris. 'It's you.'

'It's me.'

'Of course it is. How are you, then?'

'I'm fine.' Saying it to Doris's round, homely face, he felt it. He felt fine. 'How are you?'

'Oh, you know.'

'And your mum?'

'Much as usual. Can't complain.'

'Mustn't grumble,' Mrs Belcher chimed in glumly.

Troy grinned at Doris. 'Still got 'em both then? The legs? Flo said you'd had to take one of them in for repairs.'

'Part-exchanged it for a newer model, didn't I!' She lifted her cotton skirt to the knee and danced a little jig. 'See the difference?'

'Er – nope!'

Doris laughed, a rich, throaty chuckle. 'You're right! Gave me a bit of elastic support and put me on the waiting list, didn't they? Still,' she winked, 'it could be worse.'

'Count your blessings?' Troy suggested.

'There's always someone worse off,' mourned Mrs Belcher. Troy would have bet even money that the Twins from Hell were as good as gold when they were at home. But their gran was so expecting the worst, it must seem a pity to disappoint her.

'Look on the bright side,' offered Troy.

Mrs Belcher pursed her lips till they looked as if they'd been sewn together, and nodded.

Doris smothered a giggle. 'Now I'm all behind, like the donkey's tail. Where's my pencil?' The shop bell jangled. 'And here's Captain Peasgrove come for his packed lunch. Can you see to it, Troy? Twenty-four, and nine is thirty-three . . .'

Like he'd never been away.

Over the days which followed Troy eased himself back into the familiar pattern of Life in Elm Green, the way he'd always known it. He couldn't imagine Flo and Stan living their lives any differently without him there. Yet somehow, without any effort, they made a space for him to slip into which could be any size or shape he wanted it to be.

Flo cooked sausage and mash and baked beans; shepherd's pie with proper home-made gravy; fish fingers and chips. Trying to tempt him with all his old favourites. Chocolate semolina . . . apple crumble and custard . . . bread and butter pudding. Troy would eat a mouthful or two to please her, then sit pushing the rest round his plate. Flo never complained.

Days passed and merged into one another in his memory, berries ripening, grasses dying, trails of fluffy, white old man's beard in the hedgerows. Bright conkers nestled among the growing drifts of autumn leaves. Tractors strewed the lanes with gobbets of mud which set hard as rocks among the potholes, turning them into an obstacle course for a boy cycling past Willow Cottage, Lark Rise and Rivendell, as golden October crept towards grey November.

Still, way down inside, lay a deep-rooted sadness, an emptiness, from which there was no escape, however fast he rode – past the Old School House and Sebastopol Terrace, noting the changes in each garden, day by day.

Captain Peasgrove's Westward Ho! was always the first and best-prepared for winter: lawn mown and edged, hedges clipped, flower beds dug over as if the reds, whites and blues of summer had never been. While gentle Miss Moffatt, at Dove Cottage next door, could never bear to root up a single sodden marigold while it still showed willing. The birds grew fat on the seed-heads in her garden and the cats, Dusty and Daisy, grew fat on the birds which kept coming back for more. Now and then they laid out a small feathered tribute on the doorstep, to show their mistress they were truly grateful.

Past Witzend and Alma Villas . . .

It was like he was living his life in shades of grey. And no one knew how he felt. No one at all. 'If you're not busy, Troy,' Stan would say, 'I'd be glad of a hand for a bit.'

So he helped lift and bag the last of the potato crop, and footed the ladder while Stan cleared the gutters of autumn leaves. Together they stripped the apple trees, picked out the perfect fruit, wrapped each one in paper and laid them in boxes in the attic, though Flo said it was scarcely worth the trouble, what with apples being so cheap from the wholesaler these days. Stan said it was no trouble and what a wicked waste it would be to leave them for the pheasants. And Flo had to agree that, come Christmas, the flavour wouldn't compare.

Together they took down the beansticks (saving the best of the plump, pink-and-purple seeds for planting next year), tied the sticks in bundles and stashed them away in the roof of the shed.

And it was good for a while, working with his hands, not thinking too hard. Then the black mood would come on him again. A deep, deep sadness. An emptiness he didn't want to talk about. He tried not even to think about it, but it was always there.

Dad would make it right. All he had to do was hang on in there.

He never asked when Dad was supposed to be coming to fetch him away. Just in case it turned out he couldn't make it after all.

One evening there was a storm and all the lights went out. By candlelight Flo carried on sewing and Stan and Troy went on preparing sloes for sloe gin, patiently pricking each one all over with a needle. Outside the gale howled and the rain lashed at the windows, but inside Troy could hear the ticking of the clock, the crackling of the fire and the rhythm of his own breathing. Next morning he walked with Stan along the beach collecting sackfuls of the seaweed flung up by the waves to add to the compost heap.

First time he'd been down there since that morning when he saw the little ship bobbing and dipping over the waves towards him. If there ever had been a ship. The world of the mead-hall and Beowulf had begun to seem no more than the distant memory of a dream.

He'd had no more dreams of Beowulf, or Grendel. Not that he could remember. Now there were other dreams. It was OK during the day, so long as he kept moving, never looking back, past Number One, Elm Green . . . Australia Farm . . . He recited the names like a mantra as he drifted off to sleep each night. If he forgot one, or got the order wrong, he had to start again from the beginning. But the dreams still came. Dreams he could never remember when he woke, only a yawning emptiness inside.

Why didn't Dad come? Why didn't he phone? Was it something Troy himself had done? Something that happened during that dead time he couldn't remember? Hang on in there. Keep busy. Keep moving. He got tired of cycling round and round Elm Green and branched out along the lanes and byways, through Ashfield, Upshott and Steeple Rising, fetching up one day in Seahaven, a ghost town now the season was over. The sea slapped peevishly against the quay, impatient for spring. Even Leakey's Antiques and Bye-gones was shut. A sign on the door said 'Back in ten minuets', but he wouldn't bank on it. No way Leakey would have cleared up the worthless junk that spilled out on to the pavement the moment the door was opened, not just for ten minutes. Or even ten minuets.

Troy cupped his hands round his face to shut out the light and peered in at the clutter of rusting kitchen tools, the oddments of china and boxes of picture postcards, the moth-eaten rugs and sticks of furniture past even Stan's TLC. The flotsam and jetsam of forgotten lives. Saddest of all were the old photographs: wasp-waisted women and old men with whiskers, and shy teenagers in World War One uniforms who'd probably never lived to see their twentieth birthday. Sometimes people bought them for the frames.

He cycled back via Peppercorn Lane with the late afternoon sun in his eyes, not expecting to meet anyone. There'd never been any sign of life before (nor any ghosts either) at Mrs Rainbird's.

Except once, when he'd seen a grey-haired man in a grey suit moodily picking at the flaking paint on a downstairs windowsill.

The figure standing squarely in the road ahead took him completely by surprise. He yelled, braked, swerved and nearly fell off. 'Sorry! Sorry! Sorry!' What was he supposed to be sorry for? Riding along, minding his own business. 'I wasn't expecting to see you.'

'Weren't you?' said Zoe, giving him what Flo would have called an old-fashioned look.

He thought of the times he'd stopped outside the house, thinking it was empty, wishing he could roll back time, see Mrs Rainbird in her widow's black and cherry-red Doc Martens. All the rest just a dream. Imagined Zoe now, watching him unseen from some upstairs window. He felt sick with embarrassment. 'I wasn't looking for you. I was looking at the house.'

She shrugged, disbelieving. 'It's a free country.'

The sun behind her glinted in her hair, like tiny, angry sparks of electricity. There was a sadness about her he couldn't quite pin down. It reminded him of someone . . .

'What are you staring at?' she demanded.

'Nothing,' he lied. 'I . . . er . . . I keep expecting the ghost of Mrs Rainbird to come trotting round that corner.'

Zoe glanced quickly over her shoulder. 'Do you believe in ghosts?'

'Do you?' he countered.

She gave him a long, hard stare. 'They say you died.'

'Who says?'

'People. They say you died and then you came back. Have a toffee.'

'What's this?' he said. 'Some kind of test?' It wasn't the brown bag from the shop she was offering him, or the same sort of toffees he'd sold her. He took three anyway, as payback for that trick she pulled with the charity box and the scales. 'Maybe *I'm* a ghost?'

She threw him a crooked smile. 'What was it like? Being dead?'

'I wasn't dead.'

'Flat-lining then. Was it like in the movie? All your past life—'

'I can't remember. Right?'

'Of course you can't.'

Troy looked away. 'I don't even know how it happened. I just woke up in the hospital with wires and tubes coming out of me. And this.' He pushed back the hair from his forehead, so she could take a good look at the scar.

Zoe gave a long, low whistle. 'You really don't know how you got that?'

Troy shook his head.

'Haven't they told you?'

Troy frowned, casting his mind back. There'd been a young doctor, eyes red-rimmed from lack of sleep . . . His lips were moving, but the words weren't making any sense. Troy remembered feeling sorry for him and angry with Mum, hovering on the sidelines, keeping the poor guy from his bed. 'I think they might have done,' he said. 'I still can't seem to remember.'

'Weird.'

'Yeah,' he agreed, uncomfortably. In the end, he'd had to pretend to be asleep, till Mum and the doctor both went away.

Weird or not – 'There's a party tomorrow night,' she announced. 'Do you want to come?'

'Um.' The sudden change of direction caught him wrong-footed. 'I don't know. Whose party is it? Yours?'

'Mine! As if! It's just someone's birthday. Open house. Do you want to come with me or not?'

Troy thought about it. 'I'll ask,' he hedged.

'Tomorrow night, then. Meet me at the end of the lane. Seven-thirty. See you!' She pushed the rickety gate from almost shut to one-third open, squeezed past and walked up the path towards the house.

He called after her, 'I said I don't know! You haven't even told me where the party is! I haven't made my mind up yet if I want to come!'

But Zoe had already vanished round the side of the house, leaving him standing alone. Behind him the evening sun set the sky on fire, while his shadow rushed ahead of him to lose itself in the thickening dark.

For some reason his mind drifted back to the blind man, sitting alone in the mead-hall. He shouldn't have abandoned him there.

Seven

Next day as Troy sat eating breakfast, Flo was already busy slicing onions and carrots, celery, bacon and mushrooms for lunch. 'We've got a visitor today,' she said.

Troy's heart leapt – Dad? He helped himself to another slice of toast and started buttering it before he noticed the first one lying untouched.

'Your mum.'

Troy pulled a face.

Flo persevered. 'You've been here nearly three weeks, you know.'

'I don't want to see her.'

Flo said gently, 'Troy! You must. I'll be here,' she added unnecessarily.

'She can come if she wants, I suppose. I don't have to talk to her, do I?'

'You've got to talk to her sometime,' Flo said sensibly. 'Putting it off won't make it any easier.'

Troy chewed it over. 'Is she bringing Donald with her?'

'No.'

'That's all right then. I suppose.' Another thought struck him, remembering the conversation he'd overheard on his first morning. The toast went down his throat in one solid lump. 'She's not going to try and make me go back with her?'

'Not unless you want to go.'

No way! Troy gave up on breakfast and headed for the door.

'Don't wander off too far this morning,' said Flo, as he stepped outside. 'Tell you what,' she said, reaching for a colander. 'Stan says the blackberries are ripe down on the triangle. If you'd like to fetch me some in, I can make us all an apple and blackberry pie.'

'Sounds good.' Troy took the colander, slipped on his wellies and sloped off down the garden.

Under the trees, rain overnight had brought down more leaves and turned them to a soggy pulp which deadened his footsteps. There wasn't a sound but the sighing of the wind through the branches and the odd pitter-patter of water droplets. Like the lifeblood of Grendel drip-dripping from his shattered shoulder. Drip, drip – drop. Grendel, keeping pace with him, just out of sight.

Grendel was dead, he reminded himself. But there was still a shadow lurking in the corners of his mind. Drip, drip – drop! A shadow that grew stronger, slowly taking shape . . .

It was a relief to find himself out in the open again.

The triangle was an open piece of ground between where the ditches bordering two fields met. The blackberries here were always the last to ripen and the lushest, swelling slowly, squeezing every drop of goodness out of the autumn sun and rain. So long as the frost – the devil's breath, Flo called it – didn't get to them first.

Under the grass and weeds, the briars and blackthorn and hawthorn thrusting up new shoots, the earth still remembered the time when Stan had this patch down to extra vegetables; the shape of the beds, the dip at the edges, and the paths between. The way Dad told it, Troy always imagined a small army of kids in green wellies, though Flo said they'd never been allowed to foster more than two or three at one time. All doing their bit. Weeding and harvesting. Pigs to feed and muck out, goats to milk, chicken and duck eggs to collect.

'Slave labour,' Dad called it. Smiling as he said it.

'You're right there,' Stan would grin back. 'Wore me to a shadow, you lot did. Trying to find work for idle hands. Keep you all out of mischief. It wasn't easy.'

'Best years of our lives,' sighed Dad, and meant it.

Troy's feet found their own, remembered way across the uneven ground to the place where the blackberries grew thickest. He set to work, pick-pick-pick with one hand, the other holding the colander ready to catch them. Thorns pricked and scratched at his fingers. Flurries of ice-cold, dusty waterdrops itched and stung where the brambles had drawn blood and ran down in rivulets to soak the cuffs of his coat. Any squashed, spoiled berries he ate, sucking the sweet-salt mix of juice and blood from his fingers.

How long he stayed there he couldn't have said — ten minutes? Two hours? But the colander was full, and short of tipping the berries out and starting over . . . Besides, Flo was waiting to cook apple and blackberry pie and Mum was coming to visit, probably here already. Troy sighed as he turned back towards the house. She was his mum, right? And he did love her, really he did. Of course he did. It was just so much easier when she wasn't around.

When he came out from under the trees the brightness had already gone from the morning. He'd had the best of the day. Dark clouds were building, threatening more rain. Storm-tossed gulls protested, squawking, fought back, then gave in more or less gracefully and rode the wind that carried them further inland.

And Troy felt the fear again, like spidery fingers creeping up and down his spine; the knowledge that the beast was not dead after all, but sleeping.

Mum had been careful to park the car as far up the drive as she could get, well out of the way of any customers. And boxed in the van, clean forgetting that Saturday was Stan's day for cash-and-carry. Typical Mum, trying too hard, getting it wrong.

Troy took a peek through the kitchen window. She really was doing her best to please. First time out for the Aran sweater Flo had knitted for her three Christmasses ago. Nervous fingers fluttering as she talked, like wounded butterflies lighting on her hair,

70

her earrings, her coffee spoon. *Why can't you just sit still, Mum, like other people's mothers do?*

Flo listening politely, hands clasped firmly in her lap. She'd made an effort too, cooked melt–in–the–mouth shortbread and dusted off the coffee–maker Mum had bought her, though anything but instant always gave her indigestion.

No sign of Stan.

Troy heard Mum's voice through the partly-open window. 'So much *stuff*!' she exclaimed, fingers flickering as if, like a magician, she was preparing to pluck it all out of the air. 'I mean, some of it's new. I got as far as getting it packaged up. After that, I just couldn't think what to do . . .' She shook her head, despairing.

'We'll take care of it,' Flo said quietly.

Mum wasn't listening, too busy fiddling with an earring. 'I was going to throw it out. Then I thought – villages are always having jumble sales, aren't they, in aid of the church, whatever . . . On the other hand I wouldn't like to think I'm putting you to any trouble . . .'

'It's no trouble,' said Flo. 'I'll get Stan to see to it.'

Mum took time out to rearrange her scarf. 'No problem then?'

'No problem.'

Troy kicked off his boots on the back step and pushed open the door. 'Hi, Mum.' He dumped the colander in the sink and stood watching a couple of flies trying to stagger out from among the berries, willing them to make it.

71

'Troy! Darling!'

Yuk! Sod the flies. They'd had their chance. Troy turned on the tap.

'I was just telling Auntie Flo—' Mum began brightly, the rest drowned out by the noise of running water. 'Do you have to do that now, Troy?' she yelled.

'No.' Troy turned off the tap. 'Blackberries, Mum! I picked them specially for our lunch. You are staying to lunch, aren't you? Flo's making us apple and blackberry pie – and custard?' He beamed hopefully at Flo.

'Nice,' said Mum, smoothing down her skirt, thinking, Goodbye, size ten and Hallo again, Weightwatchers. 'Troy, come and say hallo properly.'

He slouched over and offered his cheek. She leaned forward. Troy was bracing himself for kissy-kissy when Mum jerked back as if she'd been stung. 'What's happened to your face?' she demanded.

'Nothing.' His hand flew to his cheek. He could feel it, the graze left by Grendel, reminding him how close death had come, then passed on. How many days . . . weeks . . . ago? 'I told you,' he said shiftily. 'I've been picking blackberries. I've got scratches on my hands, too – look!'

'Oh! Poor you!'

'Looks like you could do with a wash!' said Flo, practical as ever. 'There's antiseptic in the bathroom cabinet, Troy, if you need it.'

'Thanks, Flo.' Troy made for the stairs.

First thing he did was examine his face in the

mirror. It was just a graze from a blackberry stem after all, a row of tiny beads of fresh blood. The whole cheek looked flushed and angry, but soap and water was all it needed. Soon done.

He left the bathroom door open and the tap gently running while he dried his face and hands, so he could creep on to the landing and listen to them talking.

'He can be very difficult, I know.'

Cheers, Mum.

'Difficult? I wouldn't say he was difficult.' *Thanks, Flo.* 'You expect him to behave as if nothing's happened? He's no trouble. We're pleased to have him here for as long as it takes.'

'I really don't like putting you to all this trouble. Donald says—'

'I said, it's no trouble.'

There was silence for a moment, broken by Mum. 'The doctor's put me on tablets again. I haven't been sleeping. And I get these tension headaches. I know I'll be fine once I can get away. Donald's trying to get the new office up and running, but he'll never manage it all on his own. Donald needs me, too. You understand?'

'We understand,' Flo said soothingly. She was trying to.

'I should be able to take Troy off your hands by Christmas.'

'Christmas!' echoed Flo.

Troy caught the disappointment in her voice. Mum didn't. 'Is that too long? The way I see it, I'll have a bit more time to spare while the office is closed over the holiday. But of course, if that's too long – or if it's a question of money—'

Flo called out, 'Troy! If you've decided to take a bath, I'm not sure the Aga will stand it at this time of day.'

Troy turned off the tap.

Downstairs he found them sitting silent on either side of the table, as if they were squaring up to arm-wrestle.

'Troy!' Mum burst out joyfully, like he'd been gone a year at least. 'I almost forgot. I brought you a present.' She fumbled in her bag and pulled out a flat, oblong package. 'Sorry. I couldn't find any proper wrapping paper.'

Troy took it and unwound the duty-free carrier bag from a video tape, unlabelled. She beamed at him. He calculated the odds on her bringing him the latest action movie. They were not good.

'Mum—' he began.

'It's Majorca!' she said proudly. 'Donald's found us a lovely house, with a patio and a swimming pool. You'll be able to see the sea from your room. We've got a jacuzzi!' she told Flo proudly.

Flo raised her eyebrows, though whether in admiration or sympathy, it was hard to tell.

Mum rattled on, 'I wanted you to see it for yourself, Troy. I said to Donald, "If Troy could only see this place—" '

'Mum! They haven't got a video.'

'Oh.' She looked vaguely round, as if there had to be a VCR lying around the place somewhere; it was just that Flo and Stan – bless them! – hadn't worked out how to use it yet.

'They haven't even got television,' said Troy, rubbing it in.

'Not since we gave up fostering,' Flo said gently. 'It didn't seem worth it, just for the two of us, though I daresay Troy misses it.'

'No, I don't,' said Troy.

'I'm sure we can find someone with a video,' Flo suggested, 'who'll let Troy watch it. It doesn't look as if it would take too long.'

'About half an hour,' Mum said stiffly.

Troy turned away. He put the video down on the dresser.

Mum's patience was wearing thin. 'Just half an hour out of your life, Troy! Is that so much to ask?'

'Time I got started on that pie!' Flo said briskly. 'If we're going to have it for our lunch. Then there'll be the leftover blackberries to freeze. Why don't you take your mum into the living room, Troy? She'll be more comfortable in there.'

Eight

Mum scooped Flo's knitting out of the way on to the living-room floor and sat down, straight-backed, knees together and feet tucked neatly to one side. The easy chair was wasted on her.

Troy chose one of the hard chairs by the table, putting half the width of the room between them.

'So!' she said brightly. 'What have you been doing?'

'Nothing much.'

She made a sympathetic face. 'Poor thing. Still a bit feak and weeble? Not up to doing much yet?'

Troy bristled. 'No. Stan's done up Dad's old bike for me. I've been riding it all over the place. Miles and miles. It's brilliant!'

She fiddled with her watch and sneaked a look at the time. 'We offered to buy you a bike last Christmas. You said you didn't want one.'

'I didn't. Not then.'

'Did you fall off?' she demanded suddenly. 'Is that how you grazed your cheek?'

'No.'

She flashed a venomous glance towards the kitchen. 'I knew she wasn't telling me everything.'

'Leave it, Mum. I'm all right!'

'Yes. Yes, of course you are.' Her hands plucked invisible bits of fluff from off her skirt. When she looked up, she was wearing her Mary Poppins face again. 'Majorca, Troy!' She beamed. 'It'll be a new start for us. We can put the past behind us. I'm flying over next weekend,' she said. 'Why don't you come with me, just to visit? We'll go shopping. You can tell me what you want for Christmas.'

'I'd rather stay here. Thank you.'

'You can't stay here for ever. I thought perhaps by Christmas . . .'

So Dad hadn't told her yet. It was down to him. 'Face it, Mum. I'm not coming to live with you. Ever.'

There was silence for a moment. Even her hands were still.

'Now you're just being silly.'

'I'm going to live with Dad.'

There was a deathly hush, then, 'You know that's not possible any more.'

'Why not? If that's what I want?'

'You know why not,' she said flatly.

'No, I don't. You don't really want me. You've got Donald. Dad's got no one except me.'

'You're doing this on purpose, Troy,' she said, tight-lipped.

'I'm going to wait here till Dad comes for me.'

'You'll be waiting a long time, then,' she snapped.

'Why's that?' Had the room suddenly turned icy cold? Or was it him?

She looked away, at the ornaments on the mantelpiece, the books on the shelf, Flo's knitting on the floor; anywhere but at him. 'Don't do this to me, Troy,' she begged.

'Why can't I live with Dad?'

She gnawed her lip. 'They told you at the hospital. You keep saying you don't know, don't remember. But I was there when the doctor told you. He spelt it out clearly enough. You can't pretend you didn't hear. Or didn't understand.'

'Understand what?'

'You know.'

'I don't.'

She gave a funny little shake of her head, then turned away, eyes down, and started rummaging in her bag. 'My tablets – do you think you could ask Auntie Flo for a glass of water?'

'What is it I'm supposed to know? Please, Mum?'

She looked him in the eye and spelled out the words oh-so carefully. 'He's never coming back for you, Troy – ever –' she took a deep breath, 'because he's dead.'

'What?' His mouth formed the word, but no sound came out. It was as if the world had suddenly stopped turning, the ticking of the clock, the sounds of Flo moving quietly about the kitchen. He was caught in a single moment outside time that seemed to go on and on and on. Then, 'Liar!' he roared.

She was shaking her head again, fumbling for her handkerchief. 'But you knew that, Troy! You knew!'

'Liar! I hate you!'

Flo appeared in the kitchen doorway, hands smeared with pastry and a smudge of flour on her cheek, looking from one to the other.

'She said Dad's dead,' Troy accused.

'Sheila!' said Flo. 'I'm not sure you should . . . the doctor said . . .'

'You tell him,' said Mum. 'Perhaps he'll believe you. I'm only his mother!' Then she did what she always did when things got too heavy. She burst into tears.

'It's not true, is it?' said Troy.

Flo hesitated, then: 'It is true, Troy,' she said gently. She was looking him straight in the eye. For a moment he almost believed her. He shook his head, 'No.'

'It is true,' she said again. 'I'm sorry.' She coiled the old wayward strand of hair back behind her ear, leaving a trail of flour. 'Dr Munro told us not to mention it,' she added nervously. 'After that poor young doctor at the hospital . . . He kept trying to tell you, he said, every way he knew, but he could see you weren't really taking it in. So in the end, he said we should let the memories come back in their own time – that's what we were supposed to do.' She glanced at Mum. 'Oh, Troy, I'm sorry.' Flo took a step towards him.

Troy was already on his feet, putting the table between them. 'How did he die, then?'

'Oh, dear. I'm not sure I'm supposed to—' Another quick glance at Mum, who was no help at all. 'It must have been very quick, Troy. Killed outright in the crash, they said. He wasn't wearing his seat belt, you see.'

Troy shook his head. 'That's crap. Dad *always* wore his seat belt. He always said there were some risks that weren't worth taking. Anyway, if he . . . if he died in the crash,' he ran his fingertips over the scar on his forehead, 'then how come he was able to visit me in the hospital afterwards?'

Flo said sadly, 'He didn't, Troy.'

'He did! Lots of times.'

'No.'

'No,' echoed Mum, muffled by a soggy handkerchief.

Troy turned on her. 'How would you know? He never came when you were there!'

Mum's face crumpled and dissolved into tears again. Flo moved across to put a comforting hand on her shoulder. 'You must have been dreaming, Troy. Wishful thinking. It was a dream, that's all.'

'I *wasn't* dreaming. I remember!' Troy ran his fingers along the scar again. 'You think because I've got this gap in my memory, you can fill it up with anything you want. But I'm beginning to remember . . .'

. . . remember waking in the night, not once, but often, to see Dad standing by the window, gazing out on to the moonlit garden. Or sitting in the half-light reading the racing page, like when he was little and had a bad dream. It was always Dad who fought off the monsters, picked them up, opened the window and threw them out, then sat with him till he fell asleep again.

In the mornings there was still a faint trace of cigarette smoke and aftershave. The nurse could smell it too. She never said anything, just wrinkled her nose and went straight to open the window.

If he'd been dreaming, then so had she.

Why were they lying to him? He couldn't believe it of Flo. Mum – yeah, why not, she'd do anything, say anything – but Flo!

Mum met his eye briefly, then dived into her bag again and came up clutching a bottle of pills. 'Do you think I could have a glass of water?' she asked pathetically.

Flo nodded, her eyes still on Troy, 'Yes, yes, of course. In a minute.'

He felt the tears welling up inside him and a lump in his throat the size of an egg. He'd choke if he didn't get out of here. He dived for the door, pushing past Flo, spinning her round so she was left staring after him as he stumbled through the kitchen and out of the door.

Then he was running, running, running free, the wind in his face and his hair damp with rain. He was halfway across the lawn before he realized he'd come out with nothing but socks on his feet.

'Troy!' Mum's voice called to him from the kitchen doorway.

Troy ran on down the path, flints nipping at his toes, twigs spiking his instep, and grit working its way into all the creases. Then he was under the trees, still running, over a carpet of fallen leaves. She'd never follow him in here, he thought, as he paused, listening: not in those brand-new high-heeled boots. But she did, swearing under her breath as her stilettos spiked up the dead leaves.

'Troy! Troy, come back. We've got to talk about this. Troy!'

'Troy!' Flo's voice echoed. 'Troy?'

The triangle was a dead end. The only way out was up – up – up! into the sheltering branches. A startled squirrel skittered out of his way. A flurry of water droplets that might have given him away fell silently on to the leaf mould below, and the tapestry of gold and brown reformed seamlessly behind him.

'Troy!' She was close, very close.

Troy crouched in the hollow between two branches and held his breath. The squirrel watched him with sad, worried eyes.

'Troy!' He could tell from the sound of her voice that she was turning, turning, trying to catch the tiniest movement in the canopy of autumn leaves above her head. 'You can't change anything by running away! He's dead, Troy. You've got to face up to that sooner or later. He's dead!'

Troy stuck his fingers in his ears. *He's not dead. If he was dead, I'd know it. I'd know!*

'Troy? Is that you up there?'

Silently he rocked backwards and forwards. *He's not dead. Grendel's dead. Grendel's dead. Beowulf killed him.*

And much help you were! snapped the blind man.

I wanted to help.

You might have got him killed.

But I didn't, he sobbed. *I didn't!*

Troy closed his eyes, finding comfort in the smell of rain-wet leaves and damp earth. When he looked again, everything was still. He was staring through an open window at the settlement. There was a pale grey, early-morning sheen about it, fringed by the darker grey shapes of the trees at the edge of the clearing. Blue-grey columns of smoke rising straight up from the cooking fires. Nobody about but the women. The men still sleeping off last night's celebration. Grendel was dead. Hold on to that.

'I thought you'd be back,' the bard said comfortably, sitting in the small room behind him.

'I've got nowhere else to go, have I?'

'Close that shutter, then,' said the blind man, 'there's nothing worth seeing out there.' The boy turned to look at him, surprised. 'My ears tell me there's no one much stirring yet. My nose tells me breakfast is still a long way off. And I can feel a draught, same as anyone who's got two eyes to see with. So close the shutter. Good! Now come over here and plump up these cushions behind me – I think the fumble-fist who made this chair was a torturer who missed his calling. Then see to the fire, let's both of us coax a bit of warmth back into our bones.'

Moodily Troy knelt and stirred the dying embers. There was precious little heat left in them and no wood put by to feed them. 'What now?' he asked.

'What now?'

'Will we be moving on?'

'What's wrong with this place?'

'Nothing. I like this place. But what's left to do here? You've told your story. Grendel's dead.'

'Grendel's dead,' the man said softly. 'Dead as a coffin nail! Dead as last week's mutton.'

Troy felt the old, nameless terror twisting again inside him.

'Grendel had a mother too,' the blind man purred. 'A mother who loved him and laid that charm on him, no blade should have the power to harm him. When Grendel fled from the heroes' hall of Heorot, did he slink back to his slimy bed among the marshlands to suffer and die alone? No! It was up into the wild hills he ran, home to the place where his mother dwelt, beneath a mountain lake so dark and drear that a deer hunted to its very brink would sooner turn and face the hounds than seek safety swimming to the other side.'

'No!' Troy felt his fear rising, morphing into a new, more terrifying shape. 'Please, no!'

'Yes! Here the cursed creature came, leaching his life's blood. And when he was stone-dead, his mother, the hell-hag, rose up through the dark, dismal waters, screaming, "Vengeance!"'

'Not for her the secret stealing through the dark. Howling like the whirlwind, she hurled down on Heorot, spreading a stink of dead-water and decay. At the sound of her passing, birds flew from their night-perches and small animals – mice, rabbits, weasels and

84

voles – bolted for their burrows and stayed shivering there till morning.

'But if the men in Heorot heard her, it seemed to them no more than the shrieking of the storm wind in the high mountains, as Beowulf and his men retired to the guest house late next evening.

'No more than a night-owl's screech, deep in the forest, as the King settled down in his own quarters, safe and secure again.

'No more than one cry among many as pigs, cattle and horses down in the village started in fear, dumb animals spooked by shadows, while the men in the great hall wrapped themselves in their cloaks and settled to sleep.

'Past the dreaming dwellings the whirlwind flew and hurled itself into the hall of Heorot.

'Men started up out of their first sleep, reaching for their weapons, but the hell-hag paid them no heed. She swept on, straight to the further wall where Grendel's arm was nailed, and snatched it down.

'Then – only then! – did she turn to face them. She had not Grendel's strength, but she made havoc in the hall.

'She had not his appetite either. One man would be enough. Which one to choose? Which one? Aeschere, the King's dearest friend, was the man marked out by Fate to die that night. With one blow, his neck was broken. The hag caught up his body as it fell, and, still clutching Grendel's arm, fled into the night, leaving the rest without the will to follow.'

'But what about Beowulf?' Troy broke in. 'Where was Beowulf?'

'I told you. In the guest house. Do you think Hrothgar would leave the man who'd saved the kingdom to rough it on the mead-hall floor?'

'And Aeschere! Wasn't Beowulf supposed to save him?'

The bard shook his head. 'Even if he had been there, Beowulf could not have saved Aeschere. It was Aeschere's fate to die that night. And no time to weep for him after. It's how a man lives his life that counts; not how long. And how he is remembered.'

'Go on, then. What happened next?'

'You interrupted. Put me off.' The old man slumped sulking in his chair.

'I'm sorry. Go on, please.'

But the silence went on and on, broken finally by a faint snore.

The boy tugged at the man's robe. 'I want to know what happens.'

'You're so smart; work it out for yourself.'

He shook the bard by the shoulder. 'Wake up! You can't go to sleep now.'

'Get off! I can sleep if I want.'

'You can't fall asleep in the middle of your own story!'

'Not my story,' the bard murmured. 'Not mine. Yours.' He settled himself more comfortably.

'My story? What's that supposed to mean?' The boy tried everything he could think of to wake him then

– prodding, shaking, tickling; whatever he did, the old man only seemed to fall into a deeper sleep. Soon he was snoring fit to wake the dead.

Troy poked irritably at the fire. A thin trickle of smoke crawled out from among the embers without the strength to hold itself upright.

He was cold. And wet through. It must have rained hard. He tried to ease the stiffness out of his joints. His socks drooped, sodden, half off his feet. He was leaning forward to take them off, wring them out, hang them over a branch to dry (not that there was much chance), when he caught a whiff of smoke again, smelling this time of tobacco.

Dad?

He heard a man's voice, softly singing, '*The men of yon forest, they asked of me, How many strawberries grow in the salt sea?*'

Troy gently parted the leaves till he could see the top of Stan's head directly below. Beside him stood a pair of wellies with clean socks draped over their tops.

'*And I answered them back with a tear in my e'e, How many ships sail in the forest?* Are you ready to come down yet?' Stan enquired, without looking up. 'Lunch is almost ready. Beef stew with carrots and mushrooms and jacket potatoes done the proper way, in the oven. Shame to let it spoil.'

No answer.

'Looks like we're in for another shower, too, pretty soon.'

Silence.

'It's all right. Your mum's gone. Want me to fetch a ladder?'

'No,' said Troy. 'It's OK. I can manage.' He clambered down from branch to branch, then swung out and let himself drop, bare feet sinking into cold, soggy leaves.

Stan took a final drag on his roll-up, threw it down and stubbed it out carefully with his foot. 'Don't be too hard on her, Troy,' he said quietly.

Troy eased his damp feet into the dry socks and wellies, ran his fingers through his hair. And said nothing.

They were walking back towards the house when Stan broke the silence again. 'It nearly broke my mum's heart when I dropped out of university to marry Flo. But we were young and we thought we knew best. We were going to help build a better world! Live the simple life, grow our own food and fill the house with kids. But . . . first my mum got sick and we had to come back here, take over the shop. And then the babies never came. So we started fostering other people's.'

'Kids like Dad.'

Stan nodded, didn't look at him. 'All the times his poor mum couldn't cope. She never would let us adopt him, though. She never stopped hoping . . . Mothers, eh? Sh!' He stretched out his arm, pulling Troy up short. Silently he pointed to a patch of sunlight where a fox, red-brown against the rust-brown leaves, lay solemnly watching them. The smell of it hung in the moist air all around, like flowering currant. Troy had seen foxes before but never so close and so totally unafraid.

Stan said softly, 'The trick is to catch the good moments as they happen.'

When Troy looked back, the fox had vanished silently away, blending into the pattern of fallen leaves.

Nine

Nothing was said about Mum's visit – or about Dad – or anything else much, over lunch. Flo kept darting him anxious glances. Stan seemed to have folded himself up mentally inside a shell of silence. Troy fixed his eyes firmly on his plate and he guessed he must have eaten what was on it, though he couldn't have told you what it was, or whether he'd had blackberry and apple pie (with or without custard) for pudding.

Afterwards Stan got up and went outside without a word while Flo started on the washing-up.

Troy found the video Mum had brought, still lying on the dresser. He picked it up, weighed it in his hand, considering, then headed outside, round the front, towards the dustbins.

The van was parked outside the shop with the back doors open and someone half inside it, dressed in jeans and serious-looking hiking boots.

'Zoe?'

She straightened up and spun round, all in one movement, missed cracking her head by a whisker and stood rubbing it anyway. 'Troy! Hi. You made me jump! Um. Are you coming to the party tonight, then?'

'Party?' said Troy, wrong-footed again; how did she manage to do that every single time? 'What party? Oh, that party. That's tonight? No. Thanks, but no thanks.'

'What's the matter? Won't they let you?'

'I didn't ask them.' He edged towards the wheelie bin. 'I told you before I didn't know if I wanted to come. And now I do. I don't.'

'Oh,' she said. Her mouth set in a prim little line. Her green eyes glittered. He braced himself for the big argument the way Mum would have staged it. It didn't come. 'Right,' said Zoe. 'OK. What's that you've got?'

Troy glanced down at the video in his hand. 'Nothing,' he said, opening the lid of the bin. 'Just some rubbish my mum left behind.'

'It's a video!'

'It's a home movie.'

'What of?'

'Who cares? Anyway, Flo and Stan haven't got a video player.'

'We have!' Zoe grabbed the tape before it could find its proper place among the trash that wasn't fit for compost. 'There's no label. Don't you even want to know what's on it?'

'Nope.'

'Well, I do.'

'OK, it's Come to Sunny Majorca, right? Mum and The Dork want me to go and live there. But I'm not going. End of story.' He still couldn't let it alone. 'They're lying to me. Trying to make me go. Making out I've got no choice.'

'Hey! Join the club! Parents! Even when they ask for your opinion, you've still got no choice in the end.'

'Donald's not my parent. He's a scumbag. And a slimeball. And I've just told you I'm not going, right?'

'Right.' She thought for a moment. 'It wouldn't do any harm to watch it through, though, would it? You could come round to mine tonight.'

'I thought you were going to this party?'

'I haven't said I will. I've got other videos we could watch, too, if you want.'

While Troy stood weighing up the pros and cons, Stan came edging crabwise out of the shop, his arms full of cardboard boxes.

'Mr Mayhew!' Zoe sang out. 'It's all right, isn't it, if Troy comes round to mine tonight, so he can watch his mum's video?'

'All right by me,' Stan nodded affably, offloading the boxes into the back of the van. Inside Troy could see more boxes, which was odd. Stan usually went to the cash and carry empty. 'If that's what you want to do, Troy.'

'Er,' said Troy, his mind running on two tracks at once.

'Of course he wants to,' said Zoe. 'Besides, he ought to. Don't you think? If his mum filmed it specially for him. Don't worry, Mr Mayhew. I'll look after him.'

'I'm sure you will.' Stan smiled. He slammed the van doors shut. 'Keep an eye on things here for a minute, will you, you two? While I fetch Flo's list for the cash and carry.'

'Are you going by Seahaven?' Zoe cut in.

'Your mum's shop; yes. Did you want a lift?'

'No,' said Zoe. 'No, I don't want a lift.'

Stan gave her a straight look. 'Right, then. Won't be a jiffy.' He vanished back inside the shop again, nudging the doorstop out of the way with his foot.

As soon as the door jangled shut behind him, 'Come on!' said Zoe. 'We haven't got much time.' She pulled the van doors open and leapt up inside.

'Zoe! What are you doing?'

'These boxes are for the hospice shop. All the clothes your mum left. I couldn't *believe* it when I heard Mum talking to Mrs Mayhew on the phone and she said to take them straight to the shop.'

'If you want to take a look, why didn't you just ask Stan?' Inside the van there seemed to be clothes flying in all directions.

'What if he'd said no? It's OK. I always get first pick when the stuff comes to ours. If it's robbing the needy that worries you,' she added, 'I always put something in the collecting box, though on the allowance I get these days . . . Shoot! Oh, shoot!'

'What's up?' One eyes still on the shop door, expecting Stan to reappear, Troy glanced inside the van at the clothes strewn every which way and Zoe thumping the flat of her hand on the side.

'This is all men's stuff, you moron! Why didn't you tell me?'

'I didn't know. I suppose we'd better put it back before Stan comes.'

'You put it back.' She scrambled out and stood sucking her hand where she'd bruised it.

Troy climbed inside the van and started clearing up the mess, cramming the clothes, willy-nilly, into the empty boxes. Then, after a bit – Why only men's stuff? he began to wonder. He held up a T-shirt, so he could see the logo. Donald's? No way. No way was Donald into Jethro Tull. The shirt was Dad's. He remembered Dad wearing it to the Bank Holiday fair. Dad's last try at keeping the family together. Coloured lights coming on against a navy-blue sky, old pop songs segueing into one another and Mum's happiness like a warm glow wrapping them round as they moved among the stalls and rides. He was still kneeling there, remembering, when Stan came out of the shop and found him.

'Come on, now,' Stan said gently. 'Come on down out of there.'

Troy stared round at the mess in the van. It looked worse now than it had when Zoe gave up on the scavenging. He looked round for her outside but she'd gone, taking Mum's video with her. 'It was Zoe,' he said, not blaming her, just trying to explain. 'She thought there might be something – her mum always lets her have first pick, she said – and she does pay for it . . . But it was all men's stuff – all Dad's. Sorry about the mess.'

'I'll clear it up.'

'All Dad's stuff.'

'Your mum didn't know what else to do with it.'

'But I thought she'd already got rid of . . .' Troy's voice trailed off helplessly.

Stan upended the nearest box, picked up a shirt, folded it roughly and tucked it back inside. Picked up another. 'Off you go now,' he said gruffly. 'I'll do this.'

Troy turned away and made for the house. It wasn't till he was back in his room that he realized he was still clutching Dad's Jethro Tull T-shirt.

He lay down on the bed and closed his eyes, thoughts pinballing around in his head.

Mum and her lies. 'He's dead, Troy.' Huh! File that along with 'I don't know where he's gone', and 'He doesn't want to see you', and 'He even forgot your birthday'! *Liar!* Two tickets for the *Cirque du Soleil* Dad had wasted, while Mum was dragging him on a spur-of-the-moment birthday visit to the zoo. Mum thinking circuses must mean animals.

She'd actually got Flo on her side, backing her up! Come to think of it, Flo had been acting oddly ever since he arrived, watching him every minute. Stan even quieter than usual, more closed in on himself. As if there were things he might have said but wouldn't, out of loyalty to Flo. Doris, too, trying just that little bit too hard. And the customers in the shop . . .

He picked up the T-shirt again.

She'd made such a big deal out of getting shot of all Dad's stuff. Minutes after he walked out she'd had the wardrobe door open, hands fluttering as if afraid at what she was about to do, then pouncing on three made-to-measure suits he'd hardly worn; after that shirts, shoes, underwear, CDs and classic LPs, books, souvenirs and videos, all crammed higgledy-piggledy into black plastic dustbin liners and ferried down to Oxfam. Who seemed less than grateful, maybe on account of the dirty socks and handkerchiefs – Mum's clear-out had been total.

So, this stuff must have come from the flat. Or that was what they wanted him to think. That someone – Mum? Why Mum? – had cleared out the flat. So why was it only clothes? Where were the photos of him and Dad together; Dad's lucky tie that still travelled curled up in his pocket to every race meeting after it got too old and stringy to wear; his signet ring; and the books they used to dip into when Troy was staying over – *Myths of the Norsemen*, *The Once and Future King* and *The Romance of Chivalry*. Where were they?

He held the T-shirt up to his face, trying to recapture the memory of that day at the fair. The flashy colours and the gloriously trashy prizes; the electric smell and deep-down throb of the generators. Hot dogs and candyfloss and feeling sick on the dodgems afterwards. Mum high as a kite and Dad just so grateful to see her happy again; seemed like he'd finally managed to do something right.

There was nothing. The shirt could have been anyone's. Or brand-new. Nice try, Mum. Close, but no cigar.

Why were they all lying to him? What really did happen during that dead time before he woke up in the hospital? He ran his fingers along the scar on his forehead, but the memory stayed firmly locked inside.

What lies had they told Dad about him? Was that the reason why he didn't come, hadn't phoned?

Why was he waiting for Dad to phone him anyway? He knew how to use the phone. If he could just hear Dad's voice, even on the answerphone . . .

Yet there was something – he ran his fingers along the scar again – something Dad had said. Then it was gone again.

He couldn't risk phoning from here. Not now he knew Flo was working for the enemy. He'd call from Zoe's.

It seemed like no more than ten minutes since he came up the stairs, but the daylight was fading fast. Time to go. 'We're on our way, Tel!' he whispered to his reflection in the mirror. The nose still didn't look right: *is this really me*? No time to think about that now.

In the kitchen Stan was pretending to read the paper and Flo was busy stirring soup on the stove. There were three places laid at the table, with cheese, butter, fruit and home-baked bread still warm from the oven.

'I 'spect I'll have something to eat at Zoe's,' Troy mumbled over his shoulder, setting a course for the door. 'Is that OK?' It always worked with Mum. Mum might moan a bit but she was always more relieved than anything that she didn't have to bother. Flo was different. He saw her turn as he reached for his coat, opening her mouth to protest, Stan shushing her with a look and a shake of his head. By then Troy had the door open.

'I'll be back,' he said. The door swung shut behind him. Alone in the gathering dark he felt good.

In control.

Ten

'Troy!' came an urgent whisper that made him jump half out of his skin. Followed by Zoe Jenkins materializing out of the hedgerow at the top of Peppercorn Lane.

'You didn't have to come and meet me!' Troy hissed back. (Why were they whispering?) 'I know where you live.'

'You're late,' said Zoe, in a more normal voice.

'Did you think I wasn't coming?'

'I knew you'd come. Here! You can have this back.' She thrust the video into his hand and dived back into the hedge.

'I thought—' he began.

'You thought what?' She was tugging fiercely at something fairly sizeable that had got itself snagged on the branches behind her.

'I thought we were going to watch videos.'

'You didn't really want to. Did you? Help me then! You grab the handlebars. I'll try and work the saddle free. I ran your mum's home movie through for you this afternoon. Got it? Good.'

Obediently he held the bike while she dusted

herself down. 'We could still,' he said, 'you know, go back to your place and watch something else, I don't mind what.'

'No we couldn't. My dad's watching some crummy detective thing that's going to go on for *hours*. So! We might as well go to that party.'

'I told you I didn't want to come. I still don't. You go if you want.' He thrust the bike at her and turned to go back the way he'd come. There were other places he could phone from. A payphone at the pub—

'Troy?'

'Yes?'

'I can't just turn up to this party on my own. Can I?'

'Can't you? Why me?'

'I don't *know* anyone else, Troy! This place is the pits. I *hate* it here with nothing to do and nowhere to go. *Please* come,' she wheedled. 'I've been *so* looking forward to it.'

Which didn't really square with what she'd said earlier, about maybe watching videos instead. Still . . .

Troy thought about it. Wherever they ended up, there was bound to be a phone somewhere around the place.

'Just for a little while?' she pouted.

'OK,' he said. 'I'll come.'

He crept up the narrow grass verge beside the drive to fetch his bike. He knew he shouldn't be doing this. No need to disturb Flo and Stan, Zoe said, not just to tell them there'd been a change of plan. Troy still felt guilty as he manhandled the bike over the gravel, trying not to leave incriminating footprints in the flowerbed.

'Tell them afterwards,' whispered Zoe, 'if it makes you feel better.' Then, while he was still getting his breath back, 'Catch me if you can, Tel.' She mounted up and started pedalling away.

'Don't call me that!' he yelled after her. 'Only my dad calls me that.'

'Sh!' Zoe glanced back at the house, freewheeling, and said nothing more till he caught her up.

'Want me to fill you in on that video? Just in case they ask questions.'

'If you want.'

'Well. It's mostly sun, sea and sangria. Bit like a time-share promo.'

'That's what Donald does. He sells time-shares and stuff.'

'Was that Donald in the powder-blue suit and panama hat? Cool. I've been trying to get my dad to buy himself a panama.'

'I told you, he's *not* my dad!'

'Whatever. Anyway, the house is pretty neat – tiled floors and bougainvillea round the door; swimming pool, patio with barbecue, sea view, et cet. Your room has its own loo and shower. You'd hardly have to see them, except at mealtimes, maybe not even then. They've got you satellite TV, a stereo and a computer.'

'Trying to bribe me,' spat Troy.

101

'So screw them for all you can get, since you're going to have to go anyway. I'd go like a shot, if it was me. It's got to be better than living in this dump.'

'I like this dump.'

They slipped off their bikes when they reached the main road and waited for a gap in the early-evening homeward traffic.

'I think it's clear now,' said Zoe.

'Go on, then,' he said.

'You OK?'

''Course I'm OK. No problem.' Must be the memory of that close encounter with the juggernaut the other day that was making him feel so sick and dizzy.

Zoe flashed him a worried look, then dashed across. From there she had a clearer view in both directions. Come on! she signalled.

Now his legs wouldn't move. Stupid. *Stupid!*

'Come on, Troy! I'll count to three. One – two – go, go, go!'

He shut his eyes, leaned hard on the handlebars, pushed the bike forward and let it carry him.

Made it by a nose, ahead of the next convoy.

His heart was still thumping. His hands were shaking uncontrollably. He turned his head away so she wouldn't see how close he was to bursting into tears.

'You OK?'

'I told you before I'm OK. Let's go.'

'You said you don't remember,' she said wisely. 'But I think you do. Deep down inside.'

'Remember what? What have they told you about me?'

'Nothing much.'

'Do you know what it is I'm supposed to remember?'

'How could I know?' She turned away. 'I wasn't there. Come on.'

They mounted up again and rode on into the gathering darkness, across the flatlands, not a hedge or a decent-sized tree in sight. Troy began to get the strangest feeling that the faster they travelled, the further they got from the place they were supposed to be going to. Till they came to The World's End, a little old pub where Dad used to take him sometimes. The landlord sold free-range eggs and freshly-killed rabbits off the end of the bar to make ends meet. Somewhere in that dark time he couldn't remember the place had been rebranded from a Dad-sort-of-place into a Donald-sort-of-place, festooned with coloured lights and the flags of all nations.

'This way!' said Zoe. She made a sharp left into the car park.

'Is it here?' Troy asked. 'The party?'

''Course not.' Zoe propped her bike against the wall and unclipped a tartan duffel bag from the back. 'I'm just going to use their loo, that's all.'

'Oh! Right.'

'I may be some time. You'd better come in and wait.'

Troy parked his bike and trotted after her. 'What do I say if—'

'If anyone asks? You'll think of something.' She glanced at him over her shoulder as she pushed open the door to the annexe. 'Maybe not. Let's see. Just say you're waiting for someone. That's true,' she insisted, as Troy made to interrupt. 'You'll be waiting for me. Tell them it's your mum's birthday. You don't have to say it's your mum you're waiting for, or that it's her birthday today. Let them fill in the gaps. Right?'

'Right.'

She sauntered off towards the Ladies.

Troy moved off in the opposite direction, following the sign marked 'Telephone'. He'd make the call and then go home. Zoe was well able to fend for herself. In the reception area he located the one phone that took real money and punched in Dad's number. At the other end he heard the phone begin to ring. And ring. And ring. *Come on, Dad, pick up the phone. Come on, come on!* The ringing went on and on. He could hear the emptiness spreading round it, a phone ringing in an empty room. No answering machine, nothing.

Troy hung up. Dad wasn't there. Of course he wasn't. Saturday night, sitting at home in front of the telly waiting for the phone to ring? That wasn't Dad's style. No way. Think. Think! Wherever he was he'd have his mobile with him. Troy lifted the receiver to his ear again, made to key in the number – and couldn't remember it. Not one single digit. As if the record had been wiped clean from his brain.

The woman behind the reception desk was giving

him a funny look. He threw her a feeble smile and turned away. He had a sudden urge to talk to Mum. His fingers were punching in the number before he knew what he was going to say. Maybe just, Hallo. Then she'd say, 'Hallo'; and maybe, 'Is that you, Troy?' They could take it from there.

The phone rang twice, then someone picked up and a man's voice answered, 'Yes?' Donald. Troy slammed down the receiver and leaned back against the wall, defeated.

There was a girl standing at the corner of the corridor leading towards the door where they'd come in. She was wearing full war-paint and not enough clothes for the time of year. And she was beckoning to him as if she knew him.

Troy sidled over and clocked the tartan duffel bag. 'Zoe?'

'How do I look?' she preened. She'd done something really bizarre to her hair. 'You didn't tell me it was fancy dress,' he said.

The look she gave him would have frozen a polar bear. 'I have to make do with the jumble, don't I? Last year's fashions – if I'm lucky. Anyway, I don't see you making much effort!' She flounced out through the swing door, leaving him open-mouthed at the unfairness of what she'd just said. He'd come out to watch a few videos, was all. Just being friendly. Just being *kind*. How was he supposed to know they'd wind up at her rotten party? Still, maybe if he tagged along he'd get another chance to use a phone.

Catching her up outside, he took up the challenge again. 'You don't have to plaster that stuff on your face. Or your hair. You've got nice hair.'

'Have I?'

'Yeah. Why do you have to go and spoil it like that?'

'It'll wash out,' she said. 'Come on. It's getting late.'

They cycled on again in single file and icy silence. He wished now he hadn't made that cheap crack about fancy dress.

Suddenly, without bothering to signal, so he nearly fell off trying to brake and follow her, Zoe turned sharp left through a gateway guarded by a pair of dozy-looking stone lions. They cycled on, up a drive with evergreens banked high either side, till they came in sight of a huge, old house. A single dim light burned in the porch. The rest was in total darkness.

'Here?' he asked nervously.

'Not in the house,' said Zoe. 'The party's in the old stables round the back. That's what I was told, anyway.'

'Who by? Whose party is it?'

No answer. Still sulking. A great evening this was turning out to be – not!

As they came round the corner of the house, they could hear the thump, thump! thump, thump! of the disco beat coming from a long, low building. Inside, the party was getting into its stride. Or whatever you call it when there's no room left to do anything but bob up and down.

'Let's dance,' said Zoe.

'Let's eat,' said Troy. All he really wanted to do was find another phone. Though the buffet did look a bit special. Maybe once he'd talked to Dad . . .

'Boys!' sniffed Zoe. 'I think I'll mingle.'

Troy looked around. There had to be a phone somewhere, for heaven's sake. The place had parquet flooring, central heating, separate toilets (labelled Ducks and Drakes) and quadrophonic sound. There must be a phone. He helped himself to a can of Coke and started working his way round the sides of the room till he fetched up against a boy roughly his own age.

'Hi there,' said the boy.

'Er – hi,' said Troy. He popped open the can and sipped his drink while he waited for a gap to open in the bobbing crowd wide enough for him to slide past.

The boy looked around. 'Who are all these people? I don't know any of them.'

'Me neither,' said Troy.

'I'm Ade, by the way.'

'Troy.'

'Do I know you?'

'I don't think so.'

'Great party, Ade!' A girl about seventeen sashayed past, waving a half-bottle of vodka. 'Have a drink? I mean a proper drink. Come on, it's your birthday!'

Ade shook his head and glared at her till the tide of bodies on the dance floor scooped her up and carried her away.

'That's Sophie,' Ade said sourly. 'She's with Col.'

'Who's Col?'

'My brother Colin.' He scowled towards the DJ's podium. 'Poser! That spiel of his was past its sell-by date when Noah was in short trousers. He always spoils everything for me. The parents left him in charge. So that's his excuse for inviting all *his* friends, all his friends' friends and anyone who might, maybe, want to book a disco sometime during the next millennium, to *my* birthday party!'

'Bothered?'

'Not!' The boy laughed bitterly.

'Is there a phone around here I can use?'

Ade looked at him curiously. 'Don't you have a mobie?'

'Er.' Troy took another sip of Coke. 'Not on me. And I really do need to phone home. Do you think I could borrow yours?' he asked casually.

Ade frowned. '*I'm* not carrying. I live here, remember?'

'Ah! Of course you do. Can I use the phone in the house, then?'

'We're not allowed back in the house. Not till the parents get home.'

'They've locked you out?'

Ade was looking at him in a funny way. 'I don't know you. You don't know Col. Are you sure you're at the right party?'

'I came with Zoe.'

'Zoe? Zoe who?'

'I think I'll just get a breath of air.' Troy edged his

way past, using his elbows to work his way against the tide of dancers. 'It's getting quite stuffy in here.'

What was he doing here anyway? He never wanted to come. A chill thought struck him: what if the reason Dad didn't answer the phone was that he was already on his way? What if Dad came for him tonight and no one knew where to find him? Stupid! Dad wouldn't just shoot through; he'd wait. Dad would tell him to go on out and enjoy himself. Except he wasn't enjoying himself; he'd felt more at home in Heorot, wreathed in firesmoke and drowsy conversation with the mead-cup passing from hand to hand.

Eleven

Outside, letting the fresh air cool his face, he began to feel better. It was a clear night without a breath of wind and just a hint of frost to come by morning.

Turning away from the path that led to the front of the house and the driveway where people were still arriving, he picked his way round the back, following a path of stepping stones across a lawn. He ducked through an archway in a red-brick wall and found himself in some kind of vegetable garden.

The parents wouldn't have left Col and Ade without some way in. Just for emergencies. There had to be a way in somewhere. Ringing Dad's mobile was still the best bet, if he could just remember the number this time. '*Think of a number, any number.*' Troy smiled to himself, remembering Dad doing card tricks. He'd never explain how the trick was done, but he didn't mind doing it over and over till you'd worked it out for yourself. Used to drive Mum crazy.

A low-hanging branch brushed his cheek. The wind soughed softly through the treetops. He wasn't alone. As the music of the disco faded, he began to pick up other faint sounds in the darkness. The scrape of metal on stone, of swords and axes being sharpened. He quickened his step.

Now he could hear the jingle of harness and the soft creak of leather as men strapped on their armour.

And voices murmuring, tethered dogs snapping at one another, shaggy mountain ponies shuffling and snuffling.

In the moonlight he saw women hauling buckets from the well, filling water bottles for their menfolk, wrapping up bread and hunks of meat, ready for a journey.

Back in their room in the guest house, the bard was stirring again. 'You were gone a long time,' the old man muttered peevishly.

Troy said nothing. He tossed down the bundle of dry branches he'd collected. His feet were damp and tingling with cold.

'Did you see anyone out there?' the old man asked.

'I saw the men getting ready for a journey. The women helping them.'

There was silence now, outside.

'Where are they going?' asked Troy.

'Where do you think?'

'After the hell-hag?'

The bard nodded. 'First things first. You get on and see to that fire. My old bones are so cold, I feel like I'm ready for my grave.'

The boy found a glimmer of red among the ashes and began to feed it with bits of dry fungi and pine cones. He leaned his head close to the floor and blew gently till the flames flickered up. It was good to have something to focus on, something as vital as rekindling a fire, coaxing life back into the still-warm embers.

'Now! Listen. Do you hear them again now?' the blind man asked softly.

'I hear them.' The creak and chink of armour, the frisking of the dogs, the shuffling of the pack-ponies, and the low voices of the men.

'You want to go with them?'

'I want to know what happens.'

'Go on then.'

'Without you?'

'It's time to let your own imagination carry you. I'll wait here and mind the fire.'

Dawn was raddling the eastern sky as men, boys, dogs and ponies gathered outside the mead-hall.

The soldiers were mounting up. Women and children crowded round, passing them swords, shields and spears, offering a last swallow of mead, an extra blanket or a blessing: 'God and his holy mother keep you!' 'Thor be your shield!'

Troy, alone and unnoticed, seized the nearest pack-pony's bridle and fell into line as the war party moved out.

Pale, sickly sunbeams creeping over the land found them already beyond the forest, following the trail of blood, the black drops of Grendel's that blighted everything it touched, and the bright, brave red of Aeschere's.

Into the foothills they trudged, moving steadily upward. Onwards and upwards, up into the wild mountains. They trekked along the side of narrow gorges where the sun never shone and no birds sang. Up steep rocky paths where even the sure-footed mountain ponies stumbled, sending scree cascading down into silence. Past echoing caves and demon-haunted pools where the wind moaned and whistled and even the bravest found themselves huddling closer together.

At evening they stood on the brink of the dark tarn where Grendel had come to die. There they found Aeschere's head, ripped off and thrown away, as a cat discards the head of a dead rabbit. There, looking down into the dark, dead water, each man saw the shadow of his own death mirrored. The coils that bind, the claws that clutch. Through the evening mist Troy heard the siren spirits calling, circling round him, of the men that Grendel murdered. His head began to spin. He felt himself falling, endlessly falling, tumbling headlong into those icy waters, and cried out 'No!' But still he went on twisting and falling, till someone caught him by the arm.

The warriors standing round were suddenly silent and still. Around them the mist thickened till it was hard to tell men and rocks apart.

The bard sat slumped in his chair, his mouth half open, his sightless eyes staring.

'Wake up!' Was that his own voice he could hear? 'Wake up! Stop playing games.'

The old man's lips formed words. 'I'm cold.'

'I've got the fire going now. Soon have you warm.' He poked at the embers till the flames roared up again, fetched rugs from the bed and tucked them round the bard's frail body. 'You've got to stay awake!'

'No.' The old man sighed, a long, wistful sigh. 'I always said I could take you so far and no further.'

'But I'm not ready!'

The man's face was paling in the half-light. 'No one's indispensable. You don't need me any more.'

'I do need you! I do!' The figure in the chair was thinning before his eyes, a ghost, no more. 'Don't leave me! Not yet. Please?' He ran to the door and flung it open. 'Help me! Somebody help me, please!' His voice echoed up and down the empty corridor, 'Help!'

All around the world was trembling, walls dissolving into shadows, torches flickering and going out one by one. 'Help me!'

Out of the darkness came a voice. 'He's coming round.'

There were faces – lots of faces – bending over him, dragging him back towards the light.

He tried to fight them off.

'It's OK.'

'Settle down.'

He was lying flat on his back. Cold damp earth under him and a round, bright moon above.

Voices:

'What's the matter with him?'

'I don't know. I heard him yell. Thought the local yokels might be trying to gatecrash.'

'All I did was catch hold of his arm. I swear to God, I barely touched him. Then he fell down.'

'Who is he, anyway?'

They drew together, one many-headed monster wondering what to make of him. A tasty snack? A nice rug?

'What's going on?' The DJ, Col – Ade's brother – was standing over him. Troy ran his eyes upwards over knee-high boots, black leather strides, white ruffles and a red bandanna that had slipped down half covering one eye. All that was missing was the parrot on his shoulder.

Troy giggled. 'Yo-ho-ho!'

'What's he been drinking?' demanded Col, trying to hide his very real fear behind a show of bluster. 'What's he taken?' Silence. 'Come on, you guys! Someone must know!'

A girl said nervously, 'Should we try mouth-to-mouth, do you think?'

'Not if he's breathing already,' snapped Col. 'Get real, Chloe!'

Another voice chortled, 'Bad luck, Chloe.'

'Water!' someone muttered. 'That's what he needs – lots of water. I think.'

'You can OD on water.'

'Is that a fact? I didn't know that.'

115

'Who is he anyway?' demanded Col. He pushed his face close to Troy's and yelled the words one at a time. 'What's – Your – Name?'

'Wiglaf.' *No, that wasn't right.*

'Wicklow? Does anybody here know Wicklow?'

Negative. Heads shaking all round.

'He's just a kid. Looks like he might be one of Ade's,' the girl called Chloe said helpfully.

'Ade!' roared Col.

Someone came up with another bright idea: 'Why don't we take him to A and E?'

'What?'

'I mean we could just take him and dump him there.'

'Ade!'

'The nearest hospital must be twenty miles.'

'Each way.'

'You drive him there if you want.'

Then the birthday boy appeared, passed hand to hand like a game of Pass the Parcel, no one wanting to be caught with a forfeit. He stood swaying lightly on his toes.

'Friend of yours?' demanded Col.

Ade grunted something which might have been yes or no. 'He said he wanted to get some air.'

Troy lay for what seemed like a long, long time, feeling he ought to say something, do something, if he could only think what. Then he heard Zoe's voice picking up on what Ade had just said: '*Give* him some air, then, for heaven's sake!' Zoe elbowing useless bodies aside.

'Whoo! Here come da Slayer!' somebody murmured.

She staked him with a look, then knelt beside Troy, pushing back the hair from his damp forehead, running cool fingertips along the line of the scar which felt to him as if it must be on fire. 'He hasn't been well,' she told the muppets standing round. 'But he's all right now. Aren't you?' She waved a hand in front of him: 'Hallo-oo?'

'I'm all right,' Troy croaked obediently.

'You see?' Zoe announced, hauling him to his feet. 'I really don't know what you're all making such a fuss about.'

'Just get him out of here!' snapped Col.

'We were going anyway,' said Zoe. She handed Troy his coat. 'By the way, Col, love the gear. *So* Last Century! My mum used to be a real fan of New Romantic. But she grew out of it. Come on, Wicklow. Let's go and find our transport.'

'Sorry about that,' muttered Troy, as they pushed their bikes past the still-sleeping lions.

'Don't be. That party was totally pants. I don't know why we bothered coming.'

We? What was with this we?

'Those girls think they fart Chanel Number Five.'

Mum's favourite perfume. Troy chuckled, and began to feel better.

'You ready to ride now?'

'I can ride.'

117

They cycled side by side in the bright moonlight.

'To tell the truth,' said Zoe, 'I've never been much good at parties.'

'Me neither.'

'I always think I'm going to enjoy them much more than I ever do – know what I mean?'

'I know.'

'You know what I sometimes wonder? I wonder sometimes if anybody really enjoys them. Maybe we're all just going through the motions. Wouldn't that be bizarre?'

She was all right really, was Zoe Jenkins.

They crossed the deserted main road – no problem – and freewheeled down into the village. Then as they neared the Post Office, 'Oh, shoot!' she said. And she was gone, vanished, bike and all. He stopped and looked around. 'Zoe?'

'Sssh!' Came from the bushes at the side of the drive.

Troy saw a pale, gangling figure walking unsteadily towards him. It seemed to be using the white line down the middle of the road as a rough guide.

Troy whispered. 'What's up?'

'Shut up! I've gone home.'

The ghostly figure shambled into the light cast by the single street lamp outside the shop. It was a man, tall and thin, with a permanently worried face and rounded shoulders, as if he was carrying all the cares of the world. He teetered up to Troy. 'Hallo,' he said. 'I'm Mr Jenkins.' There was a smell of beer on his breath.

'Zoe's dad?'

'You must be Troy.'

'She – you've just missed her.'

'Ah!' The man stared down at Troy's bike, carefully putting two and two together. 'That was kind of you. Taking her home. I was coming to collect her. She said not to bother, but I thought . . . It's just that if her mother gets home before . . .' He had an unnerving way of staring at you without quite making eye contact. 'She wasn't supposed to leave me on my own, you see. Not that I mind. If I feel the need for company, I just stroll down to the local hostelry. Nobody bothers me there. Stayed longer than I meant to this evening, I'm afraid. But I'm not drunk!'

'No,' said Troy. ''Course you're not.'

'I just have trouble walking sometimes. But I'm holding my own! Yes, holding my own.' He stared vaguely round, as if surprised to find himself there. 'I was a teacher, you know, before—'

His eyes found Troy again and fixed themselves on a point just behind his left shoulder. 'You will thank Mr and Mrs Mayhew, won't you? For inviting Zoe round this evening?'

What? Troy nodded.

'Well, I'll bid you goodnight, then. Nice to have met you, Troy.'

'Um. Yeah. You too. Goodnight.'

Mr Jenkins swivelled round, lined himself up with the road markings and shambled off back the way he'd come. Behind him, Troy heard Zoe scrambling on to her bike. 'Wait a minute!' he hissed. 'What did he mean about—?'

'Can't stop now! I've got to get home before he does!' She shook off Troy's hand and pedalled away in the opposite direction from the one her dad had taken.

Twelve

Troy lay awake in the darkness, afraid to close his eyes in case he fell asleep. Afraid of what might happen if he did. For a while back then he'd even lost track of his own name. In the end he got up and, without putting on the light, searched through the drawers of the dressing table till he found the set of felt pens they'd given him in the hospital. They said drawing pictures might help him to remember. It didn't, but they let him keep the pens anyway.

Standing by the window in the moonlight, he wrote the letters T R O Y between the knuckles of his left hand.

Then he lay down again, listening to the soft rustling of the wind among the autumn leaves outside and the faint creaks inside, as if the house was turning over in its sleep. The mournful cry of an owl not far away. The sharp bark of a fox. And the sound of someone softly sobbing, heartbreakingly, on and on, till he couldn't bear it any longer.

He got up, went to the door, listened for a moment, then slipped out into the passage. When he listened again, the crying had stopped.

A board creaked under his foot and Flo and Stan's bedroom door opened.

'Troy?' Flo was standing in the doorway, wrapping her dressing gown round her.

'I couldn't sleep,' he said. 'I was going for a glass of water.'

'I could make you a cup of chocolate, now I'm up.' He searched her face for any sign of tears, but there were none. 'Or Ovaltine? Or tea. It's no trouble.'

Troy said, 'All I want's a glass of water. I'll get it.' As he fled down the stairs, he heard the bedroom door click sorrowfully shut behind her.

The moonlight poured in so brightly through the uncurtained kitchen window, there was no need to turn on the light. He filled a glass from the tap, took a first sip so it wouldn't spill, turned to go back . . . and couldn't find the stairs.

He wandered around for a while, glass in hand, up and down passages, peering into the mead-hall where men and dogs lay curled up together, snuffling, snoring and, once in a while, crying out in their sleep. Then he was outside, moving silently between the huts with their cooking fires damped down for the night; past the pigpens and the hen-coops and the ponies asleep on their feet, till he came upon the King sitting quietly in a patch of moonlight.

'You couldn't sleep either,' the King remarked.

'I went to fetch a glass of water,' said Troy, sitting down beside him. 'Do you want some?'

'Thank you.' The King took the glass, drained it and handed it back.

Troy said, 'I was afraid.'

'Afraid of what?'

'Afraid to fall asleep. Afraid of what might happen if I did.'

The King said quietly, 'Everyone's afraid of something. Afraid and alone. No one else can ever see your fear the way you do.'

Troy knew the King and Beowulf were one and the same, the way you do know things in dreams and wonder why you never realized before.

The King said, 'Fear feeds on fear. The longer you turn your back on it, the stronger it grows. The only way to be free of it is to turn and face it.'

Troy said, 'Were you afraid of Grendel?'

The King smiled. 'Of course I was afraid – before. Not afterwards.' He stretched out a hand and pushed back the hair from Troy's forehead, running his fingers along the scar. 'I'm still afraid. Afraid I might turn out to be not quite the hero you think I am. Don't worry about it. Sleep now.'

Wrapping his cloak around him, the King got up and moved silently away into the shadows.

Troy went back indoors, rinsed out the empty glass and left it to drain by the sink. Then he went back up the stairs to his room. And he did sleep, dreamlessly.

Next morning – Sunday – there was a dusting of frost on the lawn, but the temperature was rising already.

The treetops were swathed in mist. It was going to be a fine day, once the sun broke through.

Flo was off on a day trip with the church choir to some stately home or other, though it was touch-and-go for a while whether she'd make it to the minibus in time. A two-man job.

'Go on with you,' said Stan, as he helped her on with her coat. 'You've been looking forward to it.'

'That was before Troy—'

'He'll still be here when you get back. Now, where's your handbag?'

'Over here!' said Troy. 'I've got it.'

'What about your Sunday dinners? I should have got the potatoes peeled last night. I don't know what I was thinking of.'

'We'll manage,' said Stan, ushering her away from the kitchen. 'Think of Doris. How's she going to cope with her mum single-handed?' He nodded to Troy to open the front door ready.

'Well, if you're sure . . .' Flo said doubtfully, with one foot on the doorstep.

'We'll be fine, won't we Troy?' Stan smiled and waved to Doris, with her mum in her wheelchair, waiting at the end of the drive.

'Fine,' echoed Troy, closing the door behind her.

Stan caught his eye. 'I don't know about you,' he grinned, 'but I feel like I've done a full morning's work already. You fit?'

'I'm fit,' said Troy.

'Come on, then. I could do with a hand.'

Together they collected up the fallen wood from the lawn. Tomorrow, said Stan, if the weather stayed fine, might be a good day for a bonfire. 'Your dad,' he said, 'he was the Bonfire King!'

'I know,' said Troy.

After that they raked up the fallen leaves and piled them separately from the compost to rot down into leaf mould, perfect for potting up seedlings in a year or two. As he cleared Flo's tiny flowerbed at the front of the shop, Troy discovered a clump of purple primulas, fooled by the mild autumn weather into thinking spring had come, and he felt an idiotic rush of pure joy.

Somewhere Stan was singing to himself: '*Drinking buttermilk all the week; whiskey on a Sunday.*'

Slowly the mist cleared and the sun shone through, enough to warm the flagstones outside the kitchen door as they lifted out the little old pine cupboard Stan had been working on.

'All it needs now,' said Stan, 'is a bit of wire mesh to replace those cheap old door panels I had to throw away. I've got it cut to size, ready. Saved the beading so it can be tacked back in place, hide the rough edges. Off you go, then.' He offered Troy the hammer. 'Shouldn't take you more than half an hour.' He plucked a half-smoked roll-up from behind his ear. 'I'll be here if you need me.' He patted his waistcoat pockets in search of matches.

The job took a good bit more than half an hour, though Troy was too wrapped up in his work to notice. Spot on cue, Stan slid out of the patch of sunlight where he'd been pretending to doze and gave him a hand with screwing the doors back on. 'It looks good,' he said at last. 'Tacks banged in nice and straight. You've got a good eye.'

'What are you going to do with it?'

'Mrs Jenkins told Flo she's still short of kitchen furniture. Their old place was all fitted cupboards. They had to leave it all behind. Flo says she'll run up a little pair of curtains to go behind those wire panels. Something to match their kitchen. Did you happen to notice the colour?'

'Huh?' Just in time Troy remembered he was supposed to have spent last evening round at Zoe's. 'I – um – didn't go in the kitchen.'

'Not to worry. By the way, I found this in the shed this morning.'

Mum's video.

'Oh. Yes. I left it there last night. When I was getting my bike. We went for a bike ride. After we watched the video,' he lied, unnecessarily. It would have been pitch-dark if they'd watched the video first. Why on earth would they want to go for a bike ride in the dark?

All Stan said was, 'We'd better get a move on if we're going to get ourselves some dinner.'

As they were walking down to The New Inn for a takeaway, 'Stan,' he said, 'do you ever get the feeling that there's something not quite right with the world? Like it doesn't quite fit the picture you've got in your head?'

Stan thought about it. 'You've missed a season, haven't you? Gone straight from spring to autumn.'

'A bit like jet lag?'

Stan nodded. 'Takes me anything up to a week to adjust when we only alter the clocks.' He pushed open the door of the pub. They walked into a warm fug of smoke and alcohol and bodies crowded together. But it was gone half-two, everyone off to their Sunday roast, bar two old boys determinedly nursing the dregs of their pints till the bell for closing time.

'What do you fancy?' asked Stan. 'Chicken and chips? Plaice and chips? Scampi and chips? Hamburger and chips? Chips and chips?'

'Fish and chips. Please.'

'I think I'll have the same. We can eat it out of the paper. And use our fingers. Save on the washing-up.'

They sat in companionable silence while they waited for their meal. Stan ordered a pint of bitter. Troy had an orange juice and lemonade. And as he picked it up and tasted it . . . it wasn't a sudden blinding flashback like you get in the movies. It was more of a slow burn, a growing feeling of 'I have been here before.' Daylight turned to evening and the bar was slowly filled with people drinking, smoking, talking quietly. It wasn't the same bar, but close enough, same furnishings, similar fruit machine – the beer pumps and the optics and the ranks of bottles and glasses.

He'd got no memory of what film it was they'd seen that day. Only that it was pouring with rain and neither of them could think of anywhere else to go. And afterwards it was still raining, so they dived straight into the nearest pub. Troy ordered fish and chips and Dad had the steak and kidney pie. And the telly in the corner was on. Dad's face beaming across the table: 'I love this place, Tel!'

'You've been here before?'

'Nah! What I mean is – I love this kind of place. Your good, old-fashioned spit and sawdust public bar. When I was your age, Stan used to take me down to the pub and I'd imagine myself sitting in the old Saxon mead-hall; or with King Arthur's knights at the round table. Magic!'

On the television, it was time for the lottery draw. Not every head was turned towards it, but there was a definite lull in the conversation.

'Know what, Tel? I think I just might buy myself a lottery ticket next week.'

Troy disbelieving: 'You told me you'd never bet on the lottery. Never play cards for money with strangers. Never gamble more than you can afford to lose. As for the lottery, it's just another way of taxing the poor bloody workers.'

'Did I say that?'

'At fourteen million to one, you said, you've got more chance of being struck by lightning.'

'Still, if you can't break your own rules . . . Maybe I'm going soft in my old age.'

'Not you. You'll never be old.'

'Can't say I fancy the alternative.'

'What's that?'

'Dying young,' Dad grinned, turning to watch the television screen as the numbers came up.

'Maybe I feel lucky,' he said.

'That lucky?'

'Oh, ye of little faith in your old man! One chance in fourteen million is still better than no chance at all. Just one chance, for the price of another half I wasn't planning to have anyway, since I've got to drive you home ... What about you? Are you on? Or would you rather have another drink?'

Troy toyed with his empty glass, spinning things out. He shook his head: 'I couldn't drink another drop.'

'Say no more! Just don't tell your mum. If one of us does win, it's you and me, Tel, fifty-fifty, right?'

'Right!'

'You and me, Tel!'

When they finally got outside – way past the time Dad was supposed to have delivered him back home – the rain was still pouring down. Dad pulled his coat up over his head and ran to fetch the car, leaving Troy waiting in the porch.

Then – nothing. A blank.

The swish of the rain and the creeping dark ...

'Stan? Stan! I'm beginning to remember.'

But Stan was across the other side of the room, taking their empty glasses back to the bar, collecting two white-paper-wrapped bundles, piping hot.

Troy decided to save it for later, after they got home. Sitting at the kitchen table eating fish and chips out of the paper, just him and Stan together. The quiet smile on Stan's face when he told him the memories were coming back at last.

He'd reckoned without Zoe Jenkins.

Thirteen

She was perched on the drystone wall opposite the pub entrance, kicking her heels. Looking like her proper self again, hair squeaky clean and gleaming red-gold in the autumn sun. She jumped down when she saw him.

Troy turned his head away.

But Stan touched his arm and nodded in Zoe's direction.

'I don't want to talk to her, right?' muttered Troy. 'Not now, anyway.'

'You can spare her five minutes,' Stan said easily. 'I'll walk on. Pop these in the oven to warm till you come.' Without any effort he lengthened his stride, leaving Troy well behind. No choice but to break into an undignified uphill trot, or else stick his hands in his pockets and slouch over. 'What do you want, then?'

She nodded towards the pub. 'Is my dad still in there?'

'No. Is that it?' He turned away and started walking after Stan, who was already out of sight.

She fell into step beside him. 'You've got to help me, Troy!' She glanced furtively around. 'I only let him out for a minute!'

131

'Your dad?'

'Rusty, you muppet! My dad told me to take him for a walk but I was – busy. So when he barked, I just let him out in the garden instead. Then, when I went to fetch him in again, I called and called . . . ! If my dad gets home and Rusty's not there . . . I don't want him to be upset. Please, Troy? Will you help me?'

Troy thought about it. Could Zoe's dad really be such an ogre? He'd seemed harmless enough last night. More sad than anything – sad and lost.

'Well?' she demanded.

'How do I know Rusty really has run off?'

'I just *told* you—'

'You told me last night we were going to watch videos. You told Stan I was coming round to yours and your dad you were coming round to mine. All so you could go to some rubbish party you hadn't even been invited to. I don't like people who tell lies.'

'I don't tell lies. We just changed our minds, that's all.'

Oh, like that 'we', Zoe.

'I'm sorry.' She sounded like she meant it. 'That was smart of you,' she said, 'giving those hoorays an alias. So we're the only ones who'll ever know we were there. It'll be our secret, yours and mine. Who's Wicklow?'

'No one. Time's up.' They'd reached the Post Office. 'Five minutes, Stan said. I've got to go and eat.'

'Please help me, Troy! All right, then, don't. I'm sick of that dog. I don't care if he does get shot by some farmer who thinks he might be sheep-worrying. Serve him right! He never does what I say.' She turned away, fishing for her handkerchief, and gave a kind of hiccup.

Just like Mum. Troy found himself responding. 'Oh, don't cry.' He patted her shoulder. She flinched away. 'Please don't cry. I didn't say I wouldn't help.' Anyway he liked Rusty. He didn't want anything bad to happen to him. 'Look,' he said, 'I really do have to eat. Afterwards I'll help you find him.'

'Oh, thank you, Troy.' She flashed him a brave, watery smile.

'I could get Stan to—'

'No! Don't tell him!'

'Why not?'

'Don't tell anyone. Promise?'

'OK. I promise.'

'So it'll just be you and me. I'll wait for you here, shall I?'

Fish and chips slid down his throat and barely touched the sides, a thing he would have said was impossible if anyone had asked him.

'Where's the fire?' Stan asked mildly.

'Zoe's waiting. There's something I promised to help her with.' The other stuff would have to wait; the stuff about remembering. It wasn't like it was going to slip from his mind again. There'd still be time later to tell Stan about it, long before Flo came home.

★ ★ ★

133

Ten minutes from coming in the door he was walking back out again. Found Zoe perched on the seat outside, still looking tearful. 'I'm frightened something might have happened to him,' she said. 'And it'll all be my fault. What if he gets out on to the main road?'

'You go that way, then,' said Troy.

'Right!' She glanced back once, turning, trotting backwards, and saw him still standing. 'Go on!' she mouthed.

So he went, dodging out of sight the first chance he got, down the bridle path towards Drake's Hill.

Come to think of it, Drake's Hill wasn't such a bad place to start looking. From the top you could see most of the farmland round about. He took the hill at a run, the way he always raced it with Dad, scorning the path that spiralled round it.

Halfway up, he discovered how weak he still was. His legs seemed to have turned to rubber. He had to haul himself up the last bit, grabbing at tussocks of grass, determined to make it, surprised at last to find himself tumbling on to level ground.

He lay for a while, getting his breath back, watching the last thin shreds of morning mist dispersing high above.

'Quite a climb, isn't it?' said the man in the grey suit. He'd been sitting as still as the grey rocks that littered the hilltop. 'You're Zoe's friend.'

Troy sat up.

'We met last night.' Zoe's dad. *Don't mention the dog.* 'You thought I was drunk.'

Troy shook his head. 'No.' He'd seen men like Zoe's dad in the hospital, the grey men, the hollow men, shuffling along corridors or sitting staring into space, waiting for death to claim them.

Embarrassed, he turned away and scanned the fields and meadows. He'd come up here to look for Rusty. Where would he go, if he was Rusty? The beach, maybe?

The man said, 'I'm glad Zoe's found a friend at last. A dog's not quite the same.'

Troy turned his head to look at Mr Jenkins again. 'I thought Rusty was your dog?'

'Mine?' The man smiled ruefully and shook his head. 'I could never walk him. Not with these legs. Did Zoe tell you he was mine?'

'She . . . I . . .' Troy tried to think back to the words she'd actually used. 'When I asked her why he was called Rusty, she said to ask you.'

'Yes, the name was my idea.' The man smiled. 'After the cowboy in that television programme – what was it called? – Round 'em up! Move 'em out!'

'Rawhide? But that was Rowdy – not Rusty. Rowdy Yates. Clint Eastwood, right?' No way Troy could be mistaken; the programme was one of Dad's favourites.

'Oh.' The man's face fell. 'Zoe never told me.'

'She never told me the dog was hers. Why does she have to keep doing that?'

'She's unhappy.'

'Not your fault.'

'No? I suppose not.' The man turned away and sat, staring out across the sea, towards the far horizon. 'It's a fine view, isn't it? I come up here most days, climbing the dragon path . . .' His walking stick sketched a spiral in the air. 'See how it winds round and round, following the coils of the sleeping dragon? The name Drake's Hill, you see, comes from the Latin, *draco*, meaning dragon. Here the dragon sleeps, guarding his hoard of gold. A dragon loves gold as a fish loves water – as meat loves salt – as a man loves life. Disturb him at your peril!

'A hundred or so years ago, the gentleman who owned this land set out to excavate the mound. He didn't believe in dragons. But he did think there might be gold hidden – some royal tomb, perhaps – some king who fought under a dragon banner. Do you know, he couldn't get a single local man to work for him? They were too afraid of the dragon under the hill. So our gentleman–archaeologist went down to London to hire himself a gang of Irish navvies. And died of the cholera after drinking a glass of water offered to him by a woman in Seven Dials, which he was too much of a gentleman to refuse. He hoped to find the grave of Beowulf. Instead he found his own.'

'Beowulf?' Troy echoed. The ground seemed to shift under him, as if the dragon was turning in its centuries-long sleep. 'Did you say Beowulf?'

'Ah! You know the story.' The man nodded, pleased.

Troy ran his fingers along the scar on his forehead: 'I think I used to know it. I know he killed Grendel.'

'That's the bit most people have read. You probably did it in school. When you were learning about Saxons and Vikings.'

'Yes.' Why did he feel so disappointed? 'That's probably it.' But the blind man said that this was *his* story; the story had meaning for *him*. 'But then the hell-hag came, seeking vengeance – I need to know what happened next. He doesn't die, does he? The hero can't die.'

'The hero must die – or he wouldn't be human. If the hero can't die, how can he be a hero? It's how he dies that's important. *If it be now, then 'tis not to come; if it be not to come, it will be now; if it be not now, yet it will come: the readiness is all.*'

'Is that from *Beowulf*?'

'No. Shakespeare. A play called *Hamlet*. But the idea's the same; *the readiness is all*. The readiness for death.' He turned to Troy again and smiled. 'I do rattle on, don't I? Typical teacher! I've been meaning to say, if you need any help catching up with your schoolwork . . . I've got a very good translation of *Beowulf* I can lend you, if you're interested. I'll go and look it out now, shall I? – before I forget.' He heaved himself up with an effort and stood resting on his stick. 'I'd better be going anyway. See if that wretched dog's found his way home yet. He always has before.' He teetered to where the dragon path began and shuffled off down it. Little by little the green hill swallowed him up.

Fourteen

Troy eased himself up on to the rock where the man had been sitting. He could see quite a bit more from here. Still no sign of Rusty, though. Or Zoe. Not that he expected there to be. She'd probably pushed off home. Then, after the hour was up, she'd mosey on down to the Post Office so he'd find her there waiting. OK, let her wait there for a bit. It was good here. A fine, late autumn Sunday afternoon and not a living thing stirring clear round to Seahaven.

Not a cloud. Not a breath of wind. Columns of smoke hanging motionless over cottage chimneys as if they'd been painted on to the sky. The air was so still, he could catch the deep, distant murmur of the sea and the faint shush-shush of waves breaking on the shore. He could almost hear the grass grow. Round him he sensed the rocks stirring into life, becoming men again, stamping their feet, rubbing their hands, blowing a little warmth back into frozen fingers. They sat waiting for him to begin.

'Listen!' Troy began, his voice barely above a whisper. He felt a movement in the air around him, his audience leaning forward to hear. 'Listen!' He said it louder this time and his eyes caught a shimmer of movement. 'Listen, and I will tell you now how the hero descended into the very mouth of Hell!'

'Listen!' Troy closed his eyes and when he opened them again he saw the hell-hag's pool spread out in front of him, and Beowulf, fully armed, standing on the brink, waiting.

Slowly the hero turned his head, as if to say, 'Are you coming?' Then turned back again.

Troy took a deep breath: 'With one last look at the world he knew – the rocks, the sky and the shifting clouds and the faces of his friends – the hero drew his sword and leapt into the abyss.'

A rushing wind whirled round his ears, then he was plunging down, down, down. The icy water caught at his toes and slid in seconds to the top of his head. It was all he could do not to cry out with the shock and the pain of it.

Looking upward, looking back, he saw faces turning to silhouettes round the shrinking circle of light above as the weight of his armour carried him deeper, into the world below. The light dwindled to a pinprick, then nothing. Pitch-black waters eddied round him. Shadows of monsters hovered in the darkness, slithery, sightless things that found their prey by taste and touch, reaching towards him . . .

Down, down, down into the fathomless dark. His lungs were bursting, he had to breathe soon.

Where was the hell-hag? If she could live on land, she must need air to breathe. Somewhere down here there must be a pocket of air. He turned his head, searching, searching and saw a shimmer of pale light shining through the dark.

He kicked out towards it, with Beowulf beside him, shoulder to shoulder. They broke the surface together, drinking in great lungfuls of air, dragging themselves ashore in a huge underwater cave.

The air was foul, but breathable. A pale phosphorescence glowed from stalactites and stalagmites, the walls slick and glistening, towering up into nothingness, and from the piles of plunder stolen from the hell-hag's victims: the rings, the necklaces, the boar's-crested helmets, the shields inlaid with jewels and the swords tempered nine times in the fire.

In the half-light he made out the body of Grendel lying close by the water's edge, half hidden by something crouching over it. Something that moved. Something alive. Something that moaned, the sound reverberating round and round the walls and off the surface of the water. The hell-hag was crying for her murdered child.

Then came silence. An awesome stillness.

The hell-hag lifted her head and swivelled round. Troy caught his breath; she was hideous! Her yellow-green skin was covered in warts, like a toad. Her eyes were cold and dead, like those of a fish. Her mouth, like a shark's, was a wide, cruel gash, filled with row upon row of sharp, pointed teeth.

She took one look at Beowulf and she knew him!

With an eldritch shriek she flung herself at the man who'd robbed her of her son.

Beowulf was ready. His sword sang through the air – but the hag moved faster. The sword flashed again and again. And never touched her. The hell-hag was protected by the selfsame spell that she'd laid on her son.

Beowulf ducked and dodged and weaved, like a boxer, like a fencer, like a bullfighter. The hag circled round him, watching, waiting, darting forward. Thrust, duck, dodge back. And again. Too slow! The hag lashed out. Troy watched helpless as the sword went spinning from the hero's hand.

But Beowulf stood his ground and let the hag come at him again. Hadn't he killed Grendel, who had the strength of thirty men, with his bare hands?

But the hell-hag's breath was poison. Slowly she sucked the life out of him, arms clamped round him.

Troy could feel the pain in his own chest, the struggle just to breathe. Each mouthful of air Beowulf snatched only made him weaker.

No! I won't let him die! This is my story – the blind man said this is my story and I say the hero can't die – not yet. Not in this dark hole!

What Beowulf needed was a weapon. Not his own sword lying useless where it had fallen, but another sword fit for a hero, like King Arthur's Excalibur. Out of the hell-hag's plunder, he began to conjure it – he could see it already in his mind's eye. Forged by a race of giants; carved with mystic runes, proof against any evil; tempered nine times in the fire and cooled in the blood of dragons.

'Beowulf!'

Beowulf saw it. With the hag's arms still fast around him, he took one step towards her. His other foot caught her behind the heel, throwing her off balance.

For an instant he was free, free to reach out and grasp the rune-sword before . . .

. . . before the hell-hag recovered, turned, crouched and sprang, all in one, to meet her death.

Troy never saw the blow that felled her, just a brilliant flash of light and the hag slowly crumpling, as if she was tired of it all – so tired!

And a pool of blood spreading slowly across the rocky floor till it oozed over into the water.

The lake above began to seethe and bubble. The waters foamed blood red. Deep down, the watchers saw a movement . . . a brightness . . . a body rising towards them . . . Beowulf!

Welcoming hands reached out to meet him, dragging him coughing and spluttering – but triumphant! – on to dry land.

Troy lay back, exhausted, as if he'd fought the hell-hag himself. He could still feel that crushing weight bearing down on his chest. But he'd done it! Without any help from the blind man, or any words set down in a book to tell him how things should turn out. He'd made it his story.

Someone was mopping his face with a rough, warm flannel. Which was nice of them. Except that the flannel smelt of dog. He flapped it away. 'That's enough, thanks. Get off!'

The dog barked in his ear.

Troy opened his eyes. 'Rusty?' He raised his head and looked around: 'Where's Zoe, Rusty?'

Rusty pushed him back down, one paw firmly on his chest, and started washing him again with his tongue. Troy turned his head from side to side, trying to escape the relentless licking. Much more of this and he'd have no face left. With both hands he pushed the dog away and sat up.

'Rusty! Get off, you daft dog! Rusty, sit! That's it. Good dog. No, I said, Rusty, sit!' He sat ruffling the dog's ears, letting reality slide back into place around him.

The dog rested a paw on his shoulder and looked him in the eye.

Round 'em up, move 'em out, eh, Rusty? Or Rowdy. Bet you don't care what they call you. OK. Let's go find Zoe.

He set off down the dragon path with the dog padding, panting beside him until they reached the bottom. There Rusty gave a joyful yelp, leapt head first into a pile of rotting leaves and began digging furiously.

'Rusty! Rust-ee!' Leaves, twigs, pebbles and earth flew past him as he tried to catch hold of the dog's collar. 'Come on, you daft dog. We haven't got time. There's nothing there.'

Oh, but there was, there was! Some dead thing, maybe, crawling with maggots? Magic! If you're a dog.

Troy picked up a stick and started hooking leaves out of the way, so he could see where he was putting his hand before he made another grab for Rusty's collar. Something shot past his ear. He caught a glint of sunlight on yellow metal. Probably just an old bottle-top, but something made him drop his stick and turn, scrabbling in the flying earth which was already beginning to cover the thing again, until he held it safe in his hand.

It wasn't a bottle-top; it looked more like a coin. He rubbed the dirt off with his sleeve and turned it over. It was a coin, not rusted, not tarnished. Surprisingly heavy for its size. And old. Very old, you could see by the hand-cut edges and the funny little face like a kid's drawing where the queen's head ought to be. He slipped it into his pocket.

Rusty was still digging. Troy sifted through the loose earth as the dog threw it up, dirt grinding under his fingernails. He found another coin, similar to the first. And another. He grabbed a bit of flint and joined the dog, scraping more earth away.

Together they turned up sixteen, seventeen coins before Rusty sat back, tongue hanging out, with an air of Job Done.

Troy sat looking at the row of coins laid out in front of him. Then he scooped them up and put them in his pocket. He knew now what he had to do.

'Come on, Rusty. Let's go.'

They found Zoe sitting on the seat outside the shop, her bike propped against the hedge beside her.

'You said an hour,' she grumbled. 'I waited for a bit. Then I fetched my bike and went riding round to see if I could find you. You've been ages.'

'But I found him,' said Troy. 'Look.'

Zoe looked. 'Pweuh! He's filthy! Keep him away from me. What has he been rolling in? Here!' She fished the lead from her pocket and held it out to him at arm's length. 'You take him. I'll bring the bike.'

'He's your dog,' said Troy, snapping the lead on to Rusty's collar. 'You take him.' He slipped the lead over her wrist and Rusty went mad, leaping and barking, so Zoe had her work cut out to control him.

'I'll take the bike, shall I?' Troy offered.

'OK. Get down, you stupid dog! OK!'

'Thanks, Zoe!' He swung his leg over the saddle.

'Hey! I didn't say you could ride it.'

'I asked if I could take it. You said OK.'

'I didn't mean – you beast! Anyway, what's wrong with yours?'

'Nothing. I'm in a hurry.' Plus, he didn't want to bump into Stan and have to explain if he went round the back to fetch it.

'Where are you going?'

'It's a secret,' he grinned, as he scooted away, picking up speed. 'You like secrets, don't you, Zoe?'

She struggled after him, dragging an unwilling Rusty behind her. 'Tell me!' she demanded. 'If I lend you my bike you've got to tell me.'

'I'll tell you later. Promise.'

All the same, he felt bad about leaving Stan without a word. And he still hadn't told Stan how much he'd remembered. First thing he'd do when he got there, he'd phone Stan.

Fifteen

All the way to Seahaven the fear nagged him that Leakey's shop might not be open. Of course it was open. Where else was there for Sunday trippers to come in out of the cold when they found the wind on the beach blowing straight in from Siberia and everywhere else shut till Easter?

The place stank of dust and death – and Leakey.

Troy sidled to the back of the shop, doing his best not to touch anything, in case the graveyard smell rubbed off. He'd overheard a couple of guys with dreadlocks going in one day, so he'd got his opening line off pat. 'Got something for you, Leakey.'

'Mr Leakey to you, Sonny Jim.' The old man put aside the faded newspaper he'd been reading. It had this morning's date, but there was something about Leakey that made everything he touched grow old before its time.

'Mr Leakey, then.' Troy held out one of the coins. 'How much?'

Leakey took it and turned it over in his hand. 'Where d'you get it?'

'I didn't steal it, if that's what you're thinking. I found it.'

Shifty little eyes peered at him over half-moon specs.

'That's the truth.'

Leakey wouldn't know the truth if it mugged him in broad daylight. 'Fifty p,' he offered.

'Come on, that's gold. It's worth a heck of a lot more, even if you just sold it on for scrap. OK, if you're not interested, I'll have it back. Pity. There's more where that came from.'

Leakey's fingers closed round the coin. 'How many more?'

Troy, poker-faced, counted out the rest of the coins on his palm, careful to hold them just out of reach.

Leakey's eyes gleamed.

'You're right, Mr Leakey,' said Troy, scooping them together again with a shrug. 'I ought to turn them in. I expect they're treasure trove or something. My dad had a mate with a metal detector. He told me all about treasure trove. I can get the full value, if I don't mind waiting.' He turned to go.

'Ten quid the lot!' said Leakey.

'Twenty.' Troy tossed the word over his shoulder, take it or leave it.

'Twelve.'

Troy turned again to face him. 'Seventeen. That's a pound each. OK, have it your way.' Troy turned on his heel. 'Honesty's the best policy.'

'Seventeen quid, then! Cash.' Leakey mopped his face with a king-sized purple handkerchief.

Words like honesty always brought him out in a sweat.

Dad would have been proud of him. Troy didn't let the coins out of his hand till Leakey had laid out the money on the counter with trembling fingers. The coins, if they were gold, were worth a lot more, they both knew that. But seventeen pounds was more than he needed and there was just ten minutes before the last bus left. Barely time to park Zoe's bike round behind the charity shop, slipping the chain and padlock through the door handle so her mum couldn't miss it in the morning.

He caught the bus with seconds to spare and bought a ticket to the end of the run. Which gave him half an hour to relax and decide on his next move.

The train would be fastest. But then he'd have to run the gauntlet of police and social workers who lay in wait for kids his age at all the mainline stations. Runaways. He wasn't running away, he was going to find his dad and no one was going to stop him. So he hopped on another bus for a while, then switched to the tube. Sunday evening, swaying and rattling through the dark with one old bag lady for company and a couple of girls at the other end of the carriage talking what sounded like Japanese. None of them glanced at him. He might as well not have been there.

A few people hung around on the platform where he got off, each one alone, blank-faced, like zombies.

Like a zombie, he rode the escalator up to street level. There was no one to take his ticket when he reached the top. Almost no one on the street. Eddies of dust flicked at his ankles and scraps of waste paper tumbled past. All the proper shops were closed, security grilles down against ram raiders. Lights on in the kebab house and the video rental, but no customers, nor any staff either, not that he could see. Cars parked either side of the road, part of the scenery. Now and again a pair of headlights flashed past, like they couldn't get away fast enough.

He felt strange, disconnected. He had a crazy thought: what if in the end he turned out to be Wiglaf, only dreaming of being Troy?

Head up, hands in pockets, he walked on. Turned left, leaving the bright lights behind. Troy walked faster.

He was almost running by the time he reached the quiet cul-de-sac of three- and four-storey Victorian family houses, all converted into flats. He could see a light in Dad's window. Soon be there! No need to press the bell. As he ran up the steps a couple of girls were coming out, long-haired, in jeans and quilted jackets. Students, so deep in conversation, Troy was the next best thing to invisible as he slipped past them and in through the heavy entrance door before it could close behind them. He ran straight on up the stairs. The timer on the light ran out as he reached the first landing, plunging him into darkness. He pressed the next switch in passing, fingers finding it without the need to look, and continued on up.

He could hear sounds from inside the flat. Voices – sounded like a woman's voice, he couldn't make out what she was saying above the sound of the music that was playing. Not Dad's kind of music.

He rapped on the door.

The voices stopped, but not the music.

He knocked again. Silence. Then footsteps, quick and light. He heard the chain going on. The door opened a crack. A barefoot kid in supermarket jeans and a too-tight T-shirt peered out.

'Hi!' said Troy. 'Is my dad here?'

The boy frowned.

'My dad. Mr Sheridan? Ray Sheridan? I'm Troy.'

The kid looked blank.

'I'm Troy.' He tried to summon up a friendly smile. 'What's your name?'

The kid turned his head and yelled, 'Mama!'

A sallow-faced woman appeared behind him. A tiny girl in a red dress with spangles popped her head out underneath.

'Mr Sheridan?' Troy pleaded. 'Ray?'

'Rai?'

'Don't tell me you've never heard of him!'

'No!' The woman shook her head fiercely. 'Sorry, no Ing-leesh.' She held up three fingers. 'Tree day, you come. We pay. You go now. By-ee!'

The door slammed. He heard locks turning, bolts slamming into place. The music started again, much louder.

Troy slumped down on the top stair, his head in his

hands. He couldn't believe it. Dad really had moved out. He'd come all this way for nothing. Dad had upped and gone without him. But he'd promised! He'd promised! Troy wanted to cry at the unfairness of it all. Then the light went out again. He was so confused, it took him a while this time to find the switch in the dark.

He made his way slowly down the stairs. As he reached the ground floor, a door opened and a head popped out. Big, ginger hair and a tiny face all over freckles. 'Hallo, Terry!' Miss Fitzsimmons always called him Terry. On account of once hearing Dad call him Tel. Each time she did it it got harder to put her straight. That Tel was just between him and Dad. 'All on your own?' she said brightly. 'You'd better come in.'

'I – er—'

Before he could think of a reason not to, she'd whisked him inside and sat him down on the piano stool. There didn't seem to be anywhere else to sit. Miss Fitzsimmons taught piano, played in a piano bar two nights a week and never, ever, threw a book away. Dad kept promising to put up some shelves for her. Meanwhile the books went on piling up.

'Tea?' she smiled.

Troy smiled back.

'I've got Earl Grey or camomile.'

'Er.'

'Or would you prefer juice?'

'Juice would be good.'

She vanished into the kitchen alcove. Then came a

busy whirring of machinery. The juice, when it arrived, was not good. It tasted mainly of carrot, with a dash of strawberry, or possibly spinach. Spinach would account for the colour.

'I came to see Dad,' said Troy, nursing his drink, looking vainly round among the books for a couple of square inches where he could dump it and forget about it.

'Ah!' she said. 'Yes.'

'He's not there.'

'You've met our Roumanian gypsies, then. Colourful, aren't they?'

'Do you know where he's gone?'

'I – er . . .'

'He must have left a forwarding address! Or a number for me to call?'

'Ah! Excuse me. I've just remembered. I was just going to make a phone call when I . . . er. I mean when you . . . Never mind. The phone's in the bedroom.' She smiled brightly. 'Don't go away!'

As soon as the door closed behind her, Troy went looking for some place to lose his glass of juice.

His path through the maze of books took him close enough to the bedroom door for him to overhear: 'Yes, he's here now. No, he hasn't . . . What should I tell him? How much does he know?' Pause. 'All right. I'll keep him here as long as I can. But do, please, hurry.'

The door of the flat gave a soft 'click' as Troy drew it to behind him. Loud enough for her to have heard?

153

He didn't wait to find out. He wrenched the main door open and was off down the steps and into the night. Halfway down the street he felt something cold and slimy slithering down his hand and found he was still carrying the glass of gunge. So he left it in a doorway for someone to ponder over in the morning when they came to take in the milk.

There were more people about now, coming home from the movies, the pub, whatever. Enough of a crowd for him to lose himself in. A steady stream of traffic moving in both directions when he reached the main road. He stood watching the oncoming headlights, waiting for a chance to cross. Pair after pair of lights, rushing out of the darkness and the drizzling rain . . .

Except here it wasn't raining.

Still he had the impression of darkness and rain along with the rumble of traffic. Windscreen wipers going non-stop.

Headlights bore down on them, horns blaring, tyres screeching. Dad was driving like a maniac.

'Majorca?' he yelled.

'Just keep your eye on the road, Dad.' He'd kind-of thought Mum would have got round to mentioning it by now.

'She's taking you to *Ma-jor-ca*?'

'Donald's opening a new office there.'

'Donald!' Troy cocked his ears for the far-distant 'pop' of Donald vaporized by remote control. If only.

'What about me?' Dad raged. 'What am I supposed to do? Commute to the Balearics every other weekend if I want to go on seeing you? She really thinks I'm going to let her do this to us without a fight?'

'Dad! Dad, watch out! Slow down, please, Dad.'

Troy stood marooned on a traffic island, faintly surprised to find himself there, remembering . . .

They'd cruised to a stop in a lay-by, Dad half laughing, half crying, still wired, finger-combing his long yellow hair. 'You're right, Tel. That would be a fine way to solve all our problems, wouldn't it? Killing us both. That'd suit her and her fancy man just fine. Here's what I'm going to do . . .'

He thought for a moment. 'I'll go back to the court first, do it by the book, see if they can stop her taking you out of the country. If not . . . We'll do a runner! Start a new life, just the two of us. I know some people who can fix it. So if you don't hear from me for a while, don't worry. Don't even try to phone. Just go along with whatever they tell you. Keep her sweet. And trust me, right? I won't let you down. I *will* come for you . . .'

Shakily, Troy picked his way through a gap in the traffic and squeezed between the parked cars on the far side of the road.

He'd got it all wrong. He shouldn't have come here. *Don't even try to phone.* He should have stayed with Flo and Stan, kept his head down and waited, like Dad said.

The only thing to do now was go back. No need to hide any more. He'd get the bus back to the centre of town. Let the Old Bill pick him up at the station and give him a free ride back to Elm Green.

He settled down in the bus shelter to wait.

'Up!' Someone kicked his ankle. Hard. And not for the first time, by the feel of it. 'Up, up, up!'

Troy wasn't sure at first which world he was waking to. The smell of manure and leather and unwashed bodies was so strong. Then he saw it was just one body, one shapeless lump looming over him, with street lamps, parked cars and buildings in darkness parading away into the distance on either side.

'Up!' the Lump said again.

'Sorry?'

'This place is spoken for. It's mine.'

Troy stood up. 'This is a public bus stop,' he said firmly. 'I'm waiting for the bus.'

'Last bus went. Hours ago. Now, shift! I gotta get my beauty sleep.'

Troy edged round till the light was behind him, so he could look the old man squarely in his rheumy eyes.

He wasn't such an old man after all – probably not much more than forty underneath the stubble – and frightened, far more frightened than Troy was himself.

'I fought for Queen an' country an' Mrs Thatcher-gawd-bless-'er!' the Lump announced, drawing himself up more or less to attention. 'I got a right to my own space.'

'OK.' Troy held up his hands in surrender. 'No problem. I'll go.'

The man seemed suddenly to cave in. 'I s'pose there's room for both of us – just for tonight, mind! I don't mind sharing, just for one night.'

Troy went on backing away. 'If the last bus has gone,' he said. 'I'll walk.'

'Suit yourself. I was just trying to be hobsita-hostiti- friendly.' The man collapsed in a sulky heap, landing more by luck than judgement squarely on the plastic seat, and keeled sideways. 'Kids!' he muttered. 'I hate 'em!'

Troy put a good few metres between them before he turned his back. As he walked smartly away the man was already snoring.

He had a long walk ahead of him, along dark, empty streets. The blustery wind had turned to drizzling rain while he slept. Was this such a good idea? he asked himself.

The clock on the tower of the boarded-up church at the first junction showed quarter past two. The light was too dim even under a street lamp to tell the hands apart on his watch, but he guessed sometime after two would be about right. There'd be no trains now till morning and he'd be soaked through long before he reached the station. The best thing was to find shelter for the rest of the night and catch the first bus in the morning.

So he crawled in under the solitary yew tree in the graveyard, where the branches swept close to the ground and the earth was still dry. He curled himself up like a baby and fell into an uneasy sleep.

Sixteen

It was at the dead hour just before the dawn they came for him, rousting him out of his hiding place.

'Here!'

'Over here! Let's have some light here!'

'Got him!'

Kicking and wriggling he was dragged out, still surfacing out of the mists of sleep, half blinded by the flickering flames of the torches. Men with daggers drawn seized him by the arms and dragged his head roughly back by the hair: 'Is this him?'

'Wiglaf! Yes!'

'My name's not Wiglaf! Wiglaf's just what the bard called me!'

'Shut it!' Someone kicked his legs from under him. 'Speak when you're spoken to!'

'The bard's boy – yes!'

They kicked him a few more times, then dragged him upright, spinning him round to face the speaker.

'The bard's boy – yes, that's him!'

'You sure?'

'Sat right next to him, wasn't I? All through the meal. I'd know him anywhere. Wiglaf!'

'Troy! I'm Troy. I wrote it on my hand so I'd remember — look!' He tried to hold up his fist for them to see, but there was just a blue smudge across his knuckles.

Someone wrenched his arms behind him and began tying his hands behind his back. 'Whatever. You're coming with us, my lad.'

'But I haven't done anything! What is it I'm supposed to have done?'

No answer. They flung him up like so much baggage in front of one of the horsemen.

'Careful! The King said to bring him back in one piece.'

'The King — yes! The King knows who I am! He'll tell you—'

'Save it!'

Yanked upright, sitting sideways on the horse's shoulder, he was no more comfortable than he had been before. The animal was nothing but a bag of bones, and Troy without so much as a blanket to cushion him as they set off at the gallop.

'Where are we going?' he asked, his teeth jarring together with each word.

'You'll see!'

Better to keep his mouth shut till they got there, if he didn't want a chipped tooth to add to his problems.

Grey morning light crept over a ruined land. They cantered through deserted villages and past abandoned farms. Crops spoiling in the fields, or else burned to a cinder. The houses roofless, walls tumbling and blackened by fire. Great swathes of forest reduced to charcoal stumps. Small groups of refugees camped by the roadside turned their heads away from the horsemen riding by and covered their faces in despair. Except for one place, where the ruins were still smouldering and the people had enough fight left in them to hurl stones and curses.

Grim-faced, heads up, the King's men spurred their horses and rode on. The smell of burning was everywhere now, smouldering wood, blackened corn, singeing flesh. It got into your clothes and hair and eyes and skin. And with it came another, fouler stench that wormed its way deep inside, then rose up and grabbed you by the throat.

Daylight was fading when they finally came to the King's encampment, but it didn't look at all the way that Troy remembered it. The mead-hall was small and mean, covered over with a makeshift roof of thatch. Round it stood a raggle-taggle of hovels, all more or less in ruins. Not a pig or a sheep or a goat or a chicken, nor a single child in sight.

They pulled him off the horse and manhandled him inside. Those who hadn't had the chance before managed to get in a few sly kicks and jabs. Troy got one fleeting look at the King's grim face before they flung him face down on the floor. There he lay, too winded at first even to lift his head. He was aching all over, except for his hands which he couldn't feel at all, they'd tied the ropes so tight. And he still didn't know why they'd brought him here. Only that he was suddenly more frightened of the King than he'd ever been of Grendel, or the hag, or anything in his life before.

'Untie him!'

A knife sliced through the ropes. Troy sat up and began chafing the blood back into his tingling hands. He sucked at his wrist where the knife had drawn blood. 'Won't somebody tell me, please,' he begged, 'what it is I'm supposed to have done?'

The King spoke. 'You stole from the dragon's hoard.'

'Dragon?' said Troy. 'What dragon?'

'The dragon that lays waste the kingdom!'

A voice cried out: 'Call the ferryman!'

A figure in a hooded robe with Leakey's bleary eyes blinking behind half-moon specs came shuffling out of the shadows in Leakey's carpet slippers.

This is unreal, thought Troy. I must be dreaming. But the aching in his limbs and the pain in his hands as the blood flowed back – they were real enough.

'That's him!' Leakey nodded. He mopped at his nose, his eyes, and the corners of his mouth with a king-sized purple handkerchief. 'That's the boy. Seventeen gold coins he paid me. Where did he get 'em from, tell me that. Where did he get 'em, if not from the dragon's hoard?' And faded back into the shadows.

The scribe sitting in the corner taking notes, a grey man dressed in grey, shook his head sadly, wisely, and said in Mr Jenkins' voice, 'It doesn't do to disturb a sleeping dragon. I did warn him.'

Troy said shakily, 'It was just a few coins. Just lying there, for anyone to find.'

The King shook his head. 'It wasn't just anyone who found them. It was you!'

'I needed them.'

'You stole from the dragon's hoard. Now the dragon ravages my kingdom!'

'I didn't know. You mean all this . . . this wasteland . . . is down to me? I'm sorry.' Sorry didn't really seem to cover it, the houses and forests and crops destroyed; the people dead or starving. 'What can I do to make it right?'

The King said, 'Night after night the beast lays waste the land, but we can never find the place where it sleeps by day. Can you lead us to the dragon's lair? Can you find the place again?'

Troy nodded. 'I can do that.'

'You're not afraid?'

Troy thought of Drake's Hill, with the path coiling round and round. Pictured it stirring into life as a living, fire-breathing dragon. Awesome. 'I am afraid,' he said. 'But I will take you there, if I can.'

The King nodded. 'We'll leave at first light. Rest now.'

Morning came, another day without a dawn. Sunlight filtering through the film of smoke from yet another burning village. Flames flickering on the horizon.

Together they set out, the two of them, Troy and the King, side by side, trudging across the scorched, barren

163

wasteland, past ruined farms and blighted crops and filthy streams fouled by the beast.

This is my fault! Troy thought miserably. *All my fault!*

Under a midday sun that glowed blood-red through the murk, they rested. The King's knees creaked, protesting, as he sat down on the ground. 'I'm getting too old for this,' he said.

'Not you,' said Troy. 'You'll never be old.'

The King smiled and shook his head.

When they moved off again, it was Troy who led the way. How he knew which paths to take, he couldn't say. He could smell it. He could taste it. He could feel it in the tingling of his fingertips and in the fear that grew with every step he took – fear sheltering behind his shoulder, afraid to face the terror that lay ahead.

As the hazy daylight faded they came to the Dragon Hill. Bleached bones of men and beasts lay scattered around. A trail of foul slime led to a dark cave mouth.

Beowulf said: 'Is this the place?'

Troy nodded: 'This is where I found the gold.'

'Then this is where it all ends.'

There was a stirring of shadows inside the cave. A flash of green and gold. A jet of fire. The beast came slithering on its belly like a snake, undulating, slowly uncoiling, scales glistening gold, shot with sapphire blue and emerald green and ruby red. The dragon rose and stretched its wings and they were as wide as it was long. Claws at the end of them, like long, spread fingers with nails sharp as sickles.

'You don't have to do this,' said Troy.

'I am the King. This is my land.'

'What I mean is – you don't have to do this on your own. We could go back now and fetch an army.'

Beowulf smiled. 'Load the odds in my favour? And where would be the glory in that? You stay well back. Keep out of trouble. That's an order.'

The dragon preened itself in the light of the dying sun. It was, in its own way, beautiful, shimmering green and blue and gold. A jet of flame roared over their heads.

'Fire!' murmured Beowulf. 'The fire will be the worst.' There was a fleeting shadow of fear in his eyes. Then he stepped out from the cover of the rocks, beating his sword hilt against his shield, softly at first, then louder, louder. 'This is I!' he roared. 'Beowulf!' The rocks echoed: Beowulf! Be-o-wulf! 'Here I stand!' The drumming of sword on shield ran round and round, as if an army lay hidden there.

The dragon turned. Reared. Cast about, while Beowulf stood without flinching. Troy felt a spark of hope: the thing was half blind. It could only see movement. It had no way of judging distance: the eyes were set too wide apart, either side of its head, like a hare's. If you crouch down smaller the closer you get, a hare can't tell how close you are. If Beowulf could keep his head down, move fast and low while the dragon's eye wasn't on him, he might get close enough to do some real damage.

He was moving forward now, then stopped as the

dragon turned towards him. The monster paused, puzzled, its hideous head swaying from side to side. It swept the ground with a sheet of flame.

Beowulf dived for the cover of the nearest rock, his shield glowing red hot, slashing at the straps that held it with his sword.

Shieldless, he crept out and started forward again, three steps ... four ... five, before the monster sensed him. Beowulf froze, hardly daring to breathe. Then on again, only three steps this time, before the hideous head swung back towards him.

This was never going to work. Not without help. Troy scrambled to the top of the rock where he'd been sheltering. He filled his lungs and yelled: 'Hey! Hey! You old windbag! Over here! I'm over here!' He danced about and waved his arms.

The dragon turned towards him. Beowulf darted forward.

Troy dived for cover as a jet of flame roared towards him, close enough to scorch his face. He slithered over cinders and shingle.

Between the rocks he caught a glimpse of Beowulf, poised like a runner ready for the off.

Then Troy was up again. 'Hey! Hey! Hey! Over here!' This time the flames came close enough to singe his hair.

But Beowulf was getting closer.

It worked for a while, Troy a moving target, always just out of reach, Beowulf zigzagging forward. The beast was confused at first. Its great head swayed from

Troy to Beowulf and back again. But it was learning fast. It knew there was something there. Something dangerous. It flapped its wings, whipping up a cloud of choking dust. Its claws scythed deep clefts in the ground, deep enough to trip a man if he didn't keep half an eye on where he was putting his feet. All the time, Beowulf was edging closer, closer . . . He slashed with his sword at the huge leathery wing as it swept within range. Then fell, rolled under it . . . was on his feet again, within that deadly circle of fire.

Night fell, storm clouds gathering, a night without a moon or stars. By flashes of dragon-fire Troy watched as the fight dragged on. Beowulf thrust and slashed, searching for a weak spot in the armoured hide. The monster writhed and slithered, spitting fire. Then it shrieked, an ear-splitting, gut-churning sound, like metal grinding against metal.

Black blood poured from under one wing, at the soft place where it joined the body.

But Beowulf's sword was broken – shattered – useless.

The hideous head swept round and fastened its filthy teeth on the hero's neck.

Troy drew his own sword. Never mind the King's order to stay well back, keep out of trouble; he couldn't – wouldn't – let the dragon win. With a wild war cry he launched himself full tilt towards the beast, feet scrabbling on the shingle, trying to keep upright, and his heart thumping louder than a battledrum, aiming his sword-point straight for the eye of the beast.

The sword was torn from his hand by the impact. The beast screamed again and reared up, mouth opening wide, forgetting its prey.

Beowulf drew the dagger from his belt. As the dragon's head swung down again, he thrust the dagger up to its hilt into the monster's throat and fell back, exhausted.

The dying beast was toppling towards him.

Troy knew there was nothing he could do. If it was Beowulf's fate to die, there was nothing he could do to save him. Still he had to try. He was moving to help him, drag him clear, but everything seemed to be happening in slow motion . . .

The dragon falling . . .

The juggernaut thundering towards them out of the rainswept night . . . The blare of the horn, on and on, like the roar of the beast in its death throes.

The dragon endlessly falling . . .

Like the crash was never really going to happen.

The long sigh of air brakes applied too late . . .

Then the world spun round, turning topsy-turvy. The thunder crashed and the lightning flashed, over and over, electric blue. A banshee wailing filled the air.

★   ★   ★

Somewhere, bizarrely, Troy could hear a phone ringing. Someone ought to answer it, he thought as he crawled towards where Beowulf lay on the grass verge, half his body crushed under a pile of twisted metal. His eyes were closed, his face – what Troy could see of it – the colour of ashes. He laid his hand against it and the skin was deathly cold. He fumbled with the leather straps and eased off the helmet.

The King was still breathing. His eyelids fluttered. And opened. 'Did we get him?' he asked.

In that eerie blue light, Troy recognized the hero's face at last: 'Dad?'

'Hi, there. Thought you were never going to get here.' He smiled drowsily. 'So this is it, then. This is where it all ends.' There was something faintly comical in the way he looked around. 'Not quite the time or the place I would have chosen, but there you go. Life, eh? Just when you're finally getting your act together . . .'

'Don't try to talk, Dad! Just lie still. I'll get an ambulance.'

'They're here already. Looking after you. Too late for me.'

Troy looked around. Of course, that wailing sound, the flashing lights . . . He saw the police cars and the ambulance, a crumpled body lying still, with yellow-coated figures bending over it. 'Is that me?' There seemed to be blood everywhere. He felt a sudden rush of panic. 'Am I dead, too?'

169

Dad smiled. 'Not you. You're going to be fine. Gave your head a nasty crack on the dashboard, though, when we hit.'

'It's death, isn't it? The thing that I've been running from? The beast is Death.'

'It's the thing that you fear most in all the world.'

'Losing you – no!' There was one thing worse: 'Now I remember! I was leaning forward. The phone was ringing. I went to answer it just as you swerved to overtake that cyclist and I – I dropped it and—' He forced himself to put it into words: 'It was me! My fault, what happened. My fault you—'

He could feel Dad's arm round his shoulders, like when he was little and had a bad dream. 'It's OK, Tel. I'm here.' Dad chasing away the monsters while he snuggled back down under the bedclothes.

'My fault you died,' he whispered. 'If I hadn't dropped the phone— I was just trying to help—'

'What happened next?'

'I dropped the phone. It slid under your seat and—'

'– and I undid my seat-belt, so I could pick it up. I didn't have to do that. You didn't make me do it. It was a daft thing to do, just as we were coming up to a blind corner. I should have let it ring. It wasn't your fault, Tel. You might as well blame the cyclist, for not having better lights. Or the lorry-driver, for not taking a minute longer over his tea-break. If we'd seen a different film, or if it hadn't been raining . . . If, if, if! Call it Fate.' He closed his eyes.

'And you said you were feeling lucky.'

'I still do. It's a funny thing,' he mused, 'I've got a really good feeling about this, Tel. Bit like the day I bet a full week's pay on Ben Nevis at forty-to-one to win the National. I had this gut feeling . . . Best day of my life, that. Bar one.'

'What was that?'

Dad opened his eyes and grinned. 'The day you were born, of course, my son. Even if you did look like a skinned rabbit. I can see you now. And I can feel what I felt then . . . all those moments . . . everything I ever did or thought or dreamed. It's like I'm seeing the whole picture – feeling it, living it, every little moment falling into place. Death's like the last piece of the jigsaw. It's beautiful!' He closed his eyes.

'Dad? Wake up! Look at me, Dad!'

'All those moments . . . Coming to Elm Green the first time – Stan understood. Days at the races. That afternoon at the fair, with your mum. Reading to you last thing at night: *Myths of the Norsemen* and *The Sword in the Stone . . .*'

'I used to dream that you were King Arthur – or Robin Hood – or Roland, defending the pass at Roncesvalles, alone against an army – hey, Dad! Did you ever read me *Beowulf?*'

'*Beowulf?*' The eyes opened again, but they seemed to be looking through him, at something far, far away. '*Beowulf!* I used to dream of being Beowulf. Now there's a funny thing . . . I saw you lost in a dark wood.

171

There was someone with you . . .' He was drifting away again.

'The blind man – the bard. He kept calling me Wiglaf. Dad! Who was Wiglaf?'

'Wiglaf? Wiglaf, he was the boy who stood by Beowulf, right to the end, when all the rest ran away. As Beowulf lay dying, "Take the kingly torque from round my neck, Wiglaf," he said, "the seal-ring from my finger, my helmet and my armour. You are the King now. You've earned it." Everything I ever did or thought or dreamed.' His eyelids fluttered. 'Suddenly it all makes sense. Amazing!'

'Don't go to sleep on me now, Dad. Come on, wake up.'

'It hasn't been such a bad life, you know, all things considered.'

'You can't do this to me. It's not fair! You promised!'

'Sorry, Tel; when you've got to go . . . I'll see you around, yeah? Well, you know . . . If I can.' Invisible fingers brushed across Troy's forehead. Cold lips brushed his cheek. 'I don't know how I'll be fixed. Nothing changes, right? Sorry about all the times I missed.'

'That's OK.'

'It's not OK, I'm sorry. If I could just have that time back again—'

'I'm not leaving you!'

'Don't you worry about me, I'm going to be fine.' His voice was so faint Troy could barely make out the words. The light was fading, too. 'Bye Tel. Be lucky!'

172

Troy felt himself being reeled back into his own body, like a fish wriggling on a line, gasping for air. It hurt. There were bright lights and faces bending over him. 'I think he's coming round. It's all right, son, don't struggle. What's his name?'

'Troy. I'm Troy.'

Darkness closed over him again. He was drifting, floating, lighter than air. Strong hands had hold of him, lifting him up.

'I've got you, Troy. It's me, Stan. I've got you. You're safe now.'

Troy buried his face in Stan's jacket, the comforting smell of grass-cuttings and leaf-mould and hand-rolled cigarettes. 'Let's get in out of this rain,' said Stan. 'Before we're both soaked through.'

Seventeen

They sat side by side in the front of the van with the engine purring and the heating full on. Stan had brought a thermos of tea, crisps, sausage rolls, ham sandwiches, bananas, apples and a packet of mixed biscuits. The rain streamed down the windows, shutting them off from the world outside.

'How did you know where to find me?' asked Troy at last.

'Where else would you go? As soon as Zoe came and told me—'

'Told you what?'

Stan smiled faintly: 'That you'd nicked her bike.'

'I didn't nick it. I borrowed it. I left it round the back of her mum's shop.'

'Ah! We did wonder whether you were planning to cycle the whole way. She didn't come to me straight off. She thought at first you were just winding her up, trying to teach her a lesson. Then she started getting worried that you might have run away because you were frightened of getting into trouble over last night.'

'In trouble? Who with?'

'Me and Flo?'

174

Troy shook his head. 'She's mad. And she tells lies.'

'She's unhappy.'

'That's what her dad said. He's never going to get better, is he? She's watching him die, every day. Poor Zoe,' he said softly, feeling her pain more keenly, deeper than his own.

'She told me the truth, any road, when she thought you might be in trouble. I phoned Miss Fitzsimmons straight away, asked her to look out for you. As soon as she phoned back—'

'I thought she was calling Mum.'

'No sense in worrying your mum. Is that why you ran?'

'Were you worried?'

'Just a bit, when I got to Miss Fitzsimmons' place. I couldn't think where else you might have gone. It was the old soldier sleeping rough in the bus shelter who told me where to find you. He watched you go into the churchyard.'

'I thought he was asleep.'

'He could see you weren't homeless.'

'I was on my way back. But the last bus had gone.'

'Why didn't you phone me? I'd have come and collected you.'

'I didn't think. I was going to call you the minute I got to Dad's. I didn't mean for you to worry, I just didn't want you to try and stop me. Then everything went sort of pear-shaped.' Troy swallowed hard. 'He's dead, Stan.'

'Yes.'

There was a long silence that some people might have filled up with questions that had to be answered. But all Stan said was, 'I miss him. I miss him more than I can put into words, Troy. Flo, too. So we don't talk about it. And nothing else seems very important, so we don't talk about anything much any more. If it hadn't been for you, I don't know how we would have coped.'

'I didn't do anything.'

'You didn't have to. You were there.'

Another silence. Glancing sideways, Troy saw Stan's face was wet with tears. It was Stan he'd heard sobbing in the night.

'I saved his things for you, the books and photographs. A few other bits and pieces.'

'His signet ring? His lucky tie?'

'That old thing! Like a bit of chewed string. Of course I saved it.'

Take the kingly torque from round my neck, Wiglaf; the seal ring from my finger . . .

'Mum was going to throw it all away, wasn't she? Along with his clothes.'

'She'd got it all packed separate. Then she didn't know what to do. She thought you might not want to be reminded. I said, wait and see.' He paused, choosing his words before he spoke again: 'Your mum. What she really wants to say to you is "Sorry".'

'Sorry?'

'She blames herself for what happened. Your dad was late bringing you back that night. So she rang his

176

mobile. She let it ring and ring, though she knew he was probably on the road. She keeps wondering whether that was what caused the accident. Your dad trying to answer it, taking his eye off the road.'

Troy thought long and hard before he answered. 'It was nobody's fault. It was a whole lot of things coming together. Dad said call it Fate.'

Stan didn't ask him how he knew what Dad thought about it. 'Do you think you could tell her that?' he said. 'She might believe it, coming from you.'

'OK,' said Troy.

'She's going to need you.'

'I know,' said Troy, reading between the lines: Donald wasn't going to be around for ever. Majorca wasn't going to be for ever. He'd survive it.

Stan screwed the top back on the thermos. 'Anything more you want to tell me?'

'Not this minute,' said Troy. 'Later, maybe.'

Stan nodded. 'When you're ready.' He folded the sandwich wrappings and stuffed them into the glove compartment. 'What now?' he asked.

Troy said, 'Let's go home.'

They drove through empty, lamplit, rain-washed streets, the houses drifting further apart as they came to the suburbs. Clipped suburban hedges gave way to wild tangles of hawthorn and briars and bare trees stark against the velvet sky.

Through the rain-streaked window, Troy caught flashes of movement – night creatures prowling in the

177

shadows, a dog, a cat, a fox. Nothing to be afraid of. Now and again they met a car or a lorry. Once they passed a man on a bike. Mostly they had the road to themselves.

Lulled by the click–click of the windscreen wipers swinging back and forth, Troy dozed. When he woke again the rain had stopped. The moon and the stars were out. The van was purring through the sleeping countryside, wheels swishing through the puddles. Past dreaming cottages, smoke whispering from the chimneys in the moonlight. The road was a ribbon of light spinning itself out of the darkness. Rabbits on the verges snapped to attention, noses twitching, in the glare of the headlamps. A pale owl swooped low across the road in front of them.

As they crested the last hill and came within sight of the village, a pearly light was spreading all across the eastern sky. It was not dawn yet, but the day would come.

Stan was singing softly to himself: '*I wish, I wish, but I wish in vain; I wish that I was a child again . . .*'

'*But a child again I can never be,*' sang Troy, '*till cherries grow on an ivy tree.*'